Fundamentals of Philosophy & Practice

About Thea Sabin

Thea is a professional editor, writer, and Web geek. She has been practicing Wicca since she was a teenager, which was longer ago than she cares to remember. In college, she reluctantly co-founded an eclectic Wiccan-pagan student organization. After this intense lesson in Wicca 101, crowd control, interpersonal politics, academic red tape, and politely wrangling protesting fundamentalists, she took her practice "underground" and spent the next decade working with a private women's group. When that group disbanded, she sought out formal training in a British Traditional path, and over time was initiated and elevated to third degree in that tradition. Currently she and her husband run a British Traditional coven in the misty Pacific Northwest.

Thea has written for numerous pagan and nonpagan publications, and served as editor and astrology columnist for a large-circulation pagan newspaper. When she's not glued to a computer writing something, she likes to do tai chi and watch bad Hong Kong gangster movies (but not at the same time).

Fundamentals of Philosophy & Practice

WICCA *for* BEGINNERS

THEA SABIN

Llewellyn Publications • Woodbury, Minnesota

FIRST EDITION
Second Printing, 2006

Book design by Rebecca Zins

Cover design by Lisa Novak

Cover image © Digital Stock Natural Landscapes

Edited by Andrea Neff

Interior images by the Llewellyn Art Department

Llewellyn is a registered trademark of Llewellyn Worldwide, Ltd.

LIBRARY OF CONGRESS CATALOGING-IN-PUBLICATION DATA

Sabin, Thea.
Wicca for beginners : fundamentals of philosophy & practice / Thea Sabin. — 1st ed.
p. cm.
Includes bibliographical references and index.
ISBN-13: 978-0-7387-0751-8
ISBN-10: 0-7387-0751-1
1. Witchcraft. I. Title.

BF1566.S225 2006
133.4'3—dc22

2005044757

Llewellyn Publications
A Division of Llewellyn Worldwide, Ltd.
2143 Wooddale Drive, Dept. 0-7387-0751-1
Woodbury, MN 55125-2989, U.S.A.
www.llewellyn.com

Printed in the United States of America

Contents

Acknowledgments

I'D LIKE TO THANK my grandmother, who always believed I would write a book, so I finally did. She believed that the power of positive thought could conquer anything; that home-baked bread and strawberry jam were some of life's finest treasures; that astrology shows us the pattern of our full potential; that it's okay to allow yourself one cheat when playing solitaire; that the fairies and Harvey the rabbit made off with her glasses and an entire chocolate cake; and in scaring the living daylights out of little girls by reading to them in the dark about the giant spiders of Mirkwood Forest while illuminating her face in ghastly shadows with a flashlight held under her chin.

I'd like to thank some of the other mystics and shamans who have had a profound influence on me and my spiritual path—Shekinah, Otto, Eran, Akasha, Dot, Helga, Mary, Pajaro, Abuela M., Sylvana, Melanie Fire Salamander, Bestia, Star, Tom, Alicia, and Grace. Each of you has given me wonderful gifts, whether you know it or not. My love and appreciation to all of you.

I'd like to thank my guinea pigs—I mean coveners—who teach me a hell of a lot more than I teach them.

I'd like to thank Pam for inspiration, low-rise jeans, Voodoo rituals, and toothless drag queens. Everyone should be lucky enough to have a friend like you.

Most important, I'd like to thank my husband, a scientist, Zen boy, and priest whose life is a study of the arts of being rationally irrational and finding the spiritual in the mundane. He lived with me while I wrote this book, and he still loves me anyway. By that measure alone he'd be a Wiccan saint, if we had saints. I love you, baby. Chop wood, carry water.

1

What's Wicca?

RECENTLY MY HUSBAND AND I went to a coffee house to meet a man who was interested in becoming a student in our Wiccan study group. Like many Wiccans who lead teaching groups, we always arrange for our first meeting with a seeker—someone searching for his or her spiritual path—to be in a public place, for everyone's safety and comfort. Over tea, we asked the seeker why he wanted Wiccan training. We ask everyone who talks to us about training this question. If they tell us they are looking for a nature-based religion, a path of self-empowerment, a way to commune with deity, or something along those lines, we continue the conversation. If they tell us they want to hex their ex-lovers, brew cauldrons full of toxic stuff, make others fall in love with them, worship the devil, or fly on broomsticks, we tell them they're out of luck and politely suggest that they seek out a therapist.

When we asked the question of this seeker, he told us about how he had searched for information about Wicca in books and on the Internet, attended public Wiccan rituals, and visited metaphysical bookstores, but there was so much information available on the topic that he wasn't sure what was Wicca and what was not. He was also at a loss about how to separate the spiritual stuff from the rest. As he put it, "I know there's got to be a religion in there somewhere." He decided to find a teacher to help him sort it all out.

It was easy to understand why he was confused. During the last several years, Wicca and magic have stormed the American pop culture scene. We've been watching *Bewitched* for quite a while, but *Sabrina the Teenage Witch*, the Harry Potter films, *The Lord of the Rings*, *Charmed*, and *Buffy the Vampire Slayer* have spurred a new wave of seekers, despite the fact that most of these shows and films have precious little to do with real Wicca. It's gotten to the point where someone has coined the term "Generation Hex" for all of the teenagers and twenty-somethings who have been turned on to Wicca by the current magical media blitz. There are more Wicca books on the market than ever, and more than 6,000 Wicca-related Web sites on the Internet. There are Wiccan radio shows, Wiccan umbrella organizations, and state-certified Wiccan churches. And there's even Secret Spells Barbie, complete with glittery costume, cauldron, and "magic" powder. Okay, technically she's not Wiccan, but she definitely contributes to the confusion.

With all of this sudden popularity, you'd think that Wicca and magic had finally made it into the mainstream. For better or worse, this isn't true. The Wicca media glut has only given people more false, confusing, and contradictory ideas about what Wicca is. Although it's probable that more people are familiar with the word "Wicca" than ever before, there is no cohesive, accurate image of Wiccans in pop culture. Thanks to films and prime-time television, Wiccans may have "graduated" from the green-faced hag with the pointy hat to sexy women with navel rings in scanty clothes who help others with their "powers," but this is not a more accurate portrayal (there are plenty of male Wiccans, for one thing), and it's not an improvement.

Even Wiccans get confused about what Wicca is sometimes. In the Wiccan community there is a lot of discussion (okay, arguing) about what makes a Wiccan. I'm not going to jump into that fray here. Instead, I want this book to give you a broad-based understanding of Wicca so you can decide what the truth is for yourself.

For the purpose of this book, here are some definitions:

- A Wiccan is a person who is following the Wiccan religion/spiritual path and has either undergone a Wiccan initiation or has formally and ritually declared him- or herself Wiccan.
- Some Wiccans use the words "Wiccan" and "witch" interchangeably, but there are witches who do not consider themselves Wiccans. Wiccans are a subgroup of witches.
- Wiccans and witches are both subgroups of a larger group: pagans. Pagans are practitioners of earth-based

religions. Most Wiccans and witches consider themselves pagan, but not all pagans are Wiccans or witches. Christians sometimes call anyone who is not a Christian, Muslim, or Jew a pagan, but we're not going with that definition.

- In this book, when I use the term "witchcraft," I'm referring to what Wiccans and witches do: religious ritual and spell work. I use the term "Wicca" to refer to the religion itself.

So, just what *is* Wicca? There are a lot of answers to that question. Here are a few of the more widely accepted ones.

Wicca Is a "New Old" Religion

Wicca is a new religion that combines surviving folk traditions and more modern elements. It is loosely based on Western European pagan rites and rituals that have been performed for centuries—before, during, and after the time of Jesus—such as reverence of nature, observance of the cycle of the seasons, celebration of the harvest, and doing magic. Some of the structure of these old rites still survives in Wicca, but most of the religion's structure and many of its practices are more modern. Some of the framework of the religion is culled from medieval grimoires (books of magic), occult organizations such as the Golden Dawn, and techniques that today's Wiccans make up on the fly because they suit their purposes or the situation. Wicca is a living, evolving religion.

Wicca isn't the same thing as the kind of witchcraft you read about in most of the history books, but the histories of the two are intertwined. Witchcraft, in some form or another, has probably been around as long as people have been. Certainly it's mentioned in classical literature, like in the stories of Medea and Circe, and of course in documents of the early Christian Church. One of the earliest and most famous church documents about witchcraft is the *Canon Episcopi*, which had a profound and long-lasting impact on the philosophy of Christians toward witchcraft and paganism. It was incorporated into canon law in the twelfth century, but it is believed to be much older (one possible year of origin is AD 906). The *Canon* said, essentially, that witchcraft was an illusion that originated in dreams, and to believe in it was heresy, or against the teachings of the church. A famous section of the *Canon* states:

> Certain abandoned women, perverted by Satan, seduced by illusions and phantasms of demons, believe and openly profess that, in the dead of night, they ride upon certain beasts with the pagan goddess Diana, with a countless horde of women, and in the silence of the dead of the night to traverse great spaces of earth, and obey her commands as their mistress . . . but it were well if they alone perished in their infidelity and did not draw so many others along with them into the pit of their faithlessness. For an innumerable multitude, deceived by this false opinion, believe this to be true, and so believing, wander from right faith and relapse into pagan errors when they think there is any divinity or power except the one God.[1]

1. *Canon Episcopi*, in Rosemary Ellen Guiley, *The Encyclopedia of Witches and Witchcraft* (New York: Facts on File, 1989), p. 52.

The idea that believing in witchcraft and paganism was heresy persisted until the reign of Pope Innocent VIII, who issued *Summis desiderantes affectibus*, a papal bull reversing the *Canon* and stating that witchcraft *did* exist and that to perform it was heresy. Although several church letters advocating positions that would reverse the *Canon Episcopi* had been issued prior to *Summis desiderantes affectibus*, the new bull was most effective because it was published in 1484, around the time of the invention of the printing press, and attached as a prefix to the widely distributed *Malleus Maleficarum*, the infamous manual on finding, torturing, and prosecuting suspected witches, which was written by Dominican inquisitors Heinrich Kramer and Jacob Sprenger.

This bull cleared the way for the Inquisition, the European witch hunts, and the deaths of thousands of people accused of the heresy of witchcraft. And along with the *Malleus*, it helped to solidify, codify, and spread several of the ideas that came to be associated closely with medieval witchcraft. These included the notion that witches signed a pact with the devil (often solemnized by kissing his behind, something no self-respecting Wiccan would do). Of course, this made the consequences for witchcraft much more serious than they had been, and the witch hunts were born.

Pre-Christian rites were considered superstition at best, and witchcraft or devil worship at worst, so, since witchcraft was now formally considered a heresy by the church, people who were accused of performing pagan rites were prosecuted. During the witch hunts, many European pre-Christian pagan traditions died out, took on a Catholic veneer, or went underground. Some of this would have happened even without the hunts, since traditions rarely last completely intact for thousands of years. However, pockets of pagan practice and vestiges of the "old ways" survived. We see remnants of some of them today in traditions like the Morris men and Maypole dancers in England.

On one hand, this history of witchcraft and the church has nothing to do with Wicca. The "Satanic witchcraft" that the church persecuted, if it ever even existed, was a Christian heresy that included a pact with the devil, black magic, human sacrifice, and other atrocities. Wiccans do not believe in Satan, Wicca is not a Christian heresy (it's a religion unto itself), and Wiccans find black magic and human sacrifice as abhorrent as anyone else does. On the other hand, the impact that the history of Satanic witchcraft does have on Wiccans is twofold. First, the church equated even benevolent pre-Christian pagan practices, which are a root of modern Wicca, with Satanic witchcraft. Second, many people today still believe that Satanic witchcraft and paganism are the same thing.

In 1921, Dr. Margaret Murray wrote *The Witch-Cult in Western Europe,* in which she hypothesized that medieval witchcraft was in fact *not* a Christian heresy, but an organized pagan fertility cult that had survived, reasonably intact, through the Middle Ages. Her theory had great romantic appeal, but she had no proof. Her book implied that medieval witches were much more organized than they could possibly have been without phones, cars, the Internet, or even a common language (the vernacular of commoners was often different than that of nobles), and that there was more consistency between "covens" of witches than historians had previously believed. Over the years, most of Murray's theories have been discredited, and the consistency between accounts of medieval witchcraft has been attributed more to the impact of the *Malleus Maleficarum* than to survival of an intact pagan cult. If many of the inquisitors who tried witches and kept records of the trials were operating from the same manual, so to speak, they were likely to get the same results. But however fanciful Murray's ideas about witchcraft, they had a lasting effect on what would become modern Wicca, and several of them persist to this day.

In 1951, the last witchcraft law was repealed in England, which freed Gerald Brosseau Gardner to write *Witchcraft Today*, published in 1954, and *The Meaning of Witchcraft*, published in 1959—two nonfiction books that would have a tremendous impact on the Wiccan religion. Gardner was a British civil servant who was born in the late 1800s and lived most of the first half of his life abroad, working in Ceylon, Borneo, and Malaysia. He studied foreign cultures and became an expert on the kris, a Malaysian ritual knife. When he returned to England, he looked for others who were interested in esoteric teachings, and his search brought him to a Rosicrucian theater run by a group called the Fellowship of Crotona. Gardner wasn't too impressed with the theater or the Fellowship, but there was a small group of participants that intrigued him. This group later took Gardner into their confidence and told him that they were witches and that they had known him in a previous life. Gardner claims that through them he was initiated and became a witch himself.

Gardner was very interested in making sure Wicca survived. However, many of the Wiccans he knew were elderly, and young people weren't drawn to Wicca at that time, so he was concerned that Wicca would die out. He asked his high priestess if he could write a book about witchcraft to spark new interest in it. Initially she refused to let him do so, but she eventually allowed him to write a novel with witch ideas in it, called *High Magic's Aid*. Later he left her coven, started his own, and wrote *Witchcraft Today* and *The Meaning of Witchcraft*.

It's important to point out here that there was and is another type of modern witch, often referred to as "fam trad," which is short for "family tradition." Family traditions are those that have been passed down, either intact or in fragmentary form, through generations, and some of them claim to have roots that reach back to the medieval witch hunts or before. Most of them do not claim that witchcraft was an organized pagan cult, as Margaret Murray did; rather, that it consists largely of family folk magic and traditions. Most fam trad witches do not call themselves Wiccans, and their practice is often very different from what we would consider American Wicca. In fact, when Gerald Gardner's tradition appeared on the scene, it was fam trad witches who disparagingly called it the "Gardnerian" tradition. They considered Gardner's Wicca inferior since it didn't have a long history (or a verifiable history, for that matter) and because Gardner, in his zeal to preserve Wicca, was a bit of a publicity hound. The name stuck, however, and eventually lost its negative connotations. There are still lots of Gardnerian Wiccans today, and much of today's Wicca is descended from or inspired by Gardner's work—including the word Wicca itself, which he didn't invent, but popularized.

Gardner believed at least some of Margaret Murray's theory about witchcraft being a surviving pagan religion (Murray even wrote the introduction to *Witchcraft Today*). He claimed that rituals and spells his teachers had given him were fragmentary—that pieces had been lost over time—and that he took the pieces and put them back together, borrowing things from other occult sources to fill the gaps. These reconstructed rituals are still in use by Gardnerian Wiccans today. Whether he himself was initiated into an existing tradition or not, the rituals he passed on, although possibly containing old "witch" material, were not themselves an intact tradition from before the witch hunts. (This didn't stop him from occasionally letting the press believe that they were, hence the fam trad witches' distrust of him.) Wherever it truly came from, Gardner's Wicca became the root, source, or inspiration for most of the Wiccan traditions we have today.

In the 1960s and 1970s, Gardnerian Wicca, Alexandrian Wicca (a tradition that is very similar to Gardnerian Wicca), and other Wiccan and witchcraft traditions jumped the pond from the United Kingdom to the United States. Here they found fertile ground. The traditions took root and grew, and several new traditions sprouted up that were either direct offshoots of the British trads and fam trads or inspired by them.

The feminist movement of the 1960s and 1970s left its mark on Wicca too. During this time, when American women were discovering and testing their power, women (and some men too) embraced Wicca because of its worship of the Goddess and the divine feminine, something that they yearned for but didn't find elsewhere. Whereas the Wicca of Gardner's time honored both the God and the Goddess relatively equally, during this period the Goddess became more prominent in the practice of many Wiccans, and some Wiccans dropped worship of the God altogether. Other women began "Dianic" Wiccan groups, which were named after the goddess Diana and consisted only (or mostly, in some cases) of women.

Fed in part by the feminist movement and in part by good old ingenuity, eclectic Wicca began to be popular in the U.S. in the 1970s and 1980s, and it's probably the largest subgroup of Wiccans today. Eclectic Wiccans create their own rituals and practices by pulling together materials from many sources. An eclectic friend of mine affectionately calls it "shopping cart" Wicca because she equates it with rolling a cart down the aisle in the grocery store and picking from the shelves only the things she wants, likes, or can use.

In this way, eclectic Wiccans are able to customize their practice to their own personal needs and beliefs. With the rise of eclectic Wicca, Wicca truly became a "new old" religion.

Wicca Is an Earth-Based Religion

The Wiccan path is based on the earth rather than the heavens. While practitioners of many of the world's religions focus on what will happen to them after they die, Wiccans focus on participating in the cycle of life, here and now. As one of my teachers puts it, Wiccans aren't trying to "get off the wheel." What she means by the "wheel" is the "wheel of the year," a term that Wiccans use to describe the cycle of the seasons through the eight major Wiccan holidays, or "sabbats." Wiccans believe that they actively participate in turning the wheel—in nature, essentially—while practitioners of some other religions try to transcend it. Wiccans celebrate all that nature, the earth, and the physical body have to offer: the experience of life and love, sex, and even death.

A lot of the symbolism of the Wiccan religion is based on nature and earth imagery. Wiccans work with the four natural elements: earth, air, water, and fire. They see the sun as a symbol of their god, and the moon as a symbol of their goddess. They celebrate the earth's renewal each spring and its sleep each winter. Most importantly, they strive to be in tune with nature and its changes and "walk lightly" on mother earth. Many Wiccans are environmentalists or vegetarians because of their reverence for the earth, but forgetting Earth Day or grabbing a burger for lunch won't get you kicked out of the Wiccan country club.

Wicca Is Experiential

Wicca is an experiential religion. What this means is that how Wicca works in a person's life is heavily influenced by that person's experiences. There is no central church of Wicca, and no Wiccan Bible, Torah, or Koran to outline the beliefs, rules, and teachings of the religion. You learn Wicca by living it. Your experience tells you what is true, what works for you, and what you believe. We walk this path somewhat like scientists, testing things out and shifting our beliefs according to the outcomes.

Once you have experienced something, you "own" it. It is part of you. You understand it at a level that you couldn't by just reading about it. It's like skydiving. You can guess what it's like to jump out of a plane—feeling the wind buffeting your body, watching the earth rush up to meet you—but until you actually do it, you don't really know what it's like. You have not integrated skydiving into your personal repertoire of experiences. It's the same with the Wiccan religion. Until you have performed Wiccan rites or tried to do a spell, you have no frame of reference for it. You can read books like this one and guess what it would be like, but you're not a Wiccan until you do something Wiccan. Ours is a religion where actions truly do speak louder and more powerfully than words.

Does that mean that Wiccans don't learn things from books? Quite the contrary. Many Wiccans keep a "book of shadows," a collection of spells and rituals, and I know Wiccans who will run out and buy newly published Wicca books instead of groceries on payday. But Wiccan books do not tell us how to think, believe, or behave. They give us inspiration and a framework for our own experimentation with the religion.

Wicca Is a Mystery Tradition

There are certain spiritual experiences that are nearly impossible to put into words. Many of them have to do with big topics such as death, love, deity, and birth—things that are core to our existence as humans and yet otherworldly at the same time. If you've ever had a transcendent moment where you just *knew* that deity was real or you felt particularly connected to nature or the cosmos, as if every bit of you were a part of it, you have probably touched the mysteries. Mystery religions are those that create a setting or a venue where people can have an immediate experience of the reality of the divine. These paths teach that there are things that are beyond the reach of our five senses, but are nevertheless integral parts of us that we can touch directly, although the method will be different for each of us.

Each religion has its own mysteries, or revelations. Some of the Wiccan mysteries—for example, the interplay between the God and Goddess—are mirrored in our sabbat rites. When we participate in the rites, we "act out" what is happening on a cosmic level, be it the change of seasons, the union of the God and Goddess, or any other of a number of Wiccan mysteries, and for that moment we are aligned with the gods. One of the best historic, non-Wiccan examples of this is the Eleusinian Mysteries, the ancient rites of Demeter and Persephone that were held for thousands of years at Eleusis in Greece. At a certain time of year, many Greeks made the pilgrimage to Eleusis, purified themselves in the sea, and participated in the rites, which included secret revelations and teachings and built-in triggers for mystical experiences. Once they had "seen" and experienced the mysteries of the rites, they were not allowed to reveal them to others. There were many reasons for this. No two people experienced the rites the same way. Telling someone what the rites were beforehand would color and possibly ruin their experience of them. And the secrecy kept the rites sacred and protected—apart from daily life and intact for coming generations. Punishment for revealing the mysteries was severe, and the threat of it appears to have worked, because to this day no one really knows the exact content of the rituals. The secret died with the participants.

Some Wiccan mysteries unfold during meditations or dreamwork. Still others come during an "Aha!" moment when a Wiccan has been walking the path for a while, and suddenly important teachings click into place. As I said, the experience is different for everyone. But Wicca, with its focus on natural cycles and emphasis on meditation and psychic abilities, provides many opportunities to touch the mysteries of the divine and the cosmos.

Wicca Is European Shamanism

One of the best ways I've heard Wicca described is that it is European shamanism. In America, we are used to hearing stories about Native American shamans who do magic and healing for their tribes, but people of European descent have a shamanistic tradition too: witchcraft. Historian Mircea Eliade, in his classic 1964 book *Shamanism: Archaic Techniques of Ecstasy*, defines the word shaman as a person who enters an altered state of consciousness in order to take a spiritual journey to retrieve information, heal, work magic, tell the future, or commune with the dead. A shaman is more than a medicine man or a magician, although he or she is often both of these things; a shaman may also be a priest, mystic, and psychopomp (one who can move back and forth between the worlds of the living and the dead).

The concept of the world tree exists in one form or another in cultures across the globe. The world tree is a symbol for the connection between the spiritual realms and earth. The roots of the tree lie in the underworld, the trunk is the human material world, and the branches and leaves are the heavens or celestial realms. The tree can be "real" or a metaphor. The shaman travels up and down the world tree and between the spiritual and earthly realms to perform his or her tasks for the tribe or group. Shamans use many techniques to "travel" the world tree, including trance, shapeshifting, and magic.

According to Eliade, a person can be either born a shaman or made one through a "shamanic crisis" or an initiation ceremony. Children born with special features—like a caul or birthmark, certain disabilities, or unusual abilities—were considered potential shamans in many cultures. The idea was that if a person, by way of some sort of physical attribute, was different enough from the rest of the group or tribe, he or she would naturally be able to "see" and experience things that others could not, and therefore would be more suited to travel between the worlds. It makes some sense; people who are blind perceive their surroundings differently than people with sight do, and the world looks different to a person in a wheelchair than it does to one who can walk.

A shaman could be "made" if he or she went through a shamanic crisis—an event so traumatic that it changed his or her life irrevocably. The shamanic crisis could come on naturally, such as with a severe illness or near-death experience. It could also be induced from the outside by an initiation ceremony or trial.

Wicca incorporates a lot of these ideas. Wiccans are taught to be in tune with their psychic abilities. Magic circles, the sacred space of Wiccans, are said to be "between the worlds," and Wiccans "travel" between the worlds to meet the gods, get information, and heal. Wiccans often enter ecstatic or trance states in order to work magic or commune with the divine. Many Wiccans have life-altering experiences that lead them to the Wiccan path, and Wiccan groups often initiate new members in a symbolic death and rebirth ceremony meant to provide a mini-shamanic crisis and shift the initiate's perspective.

This death and rebirth stuff may sound frightening, and frankly, sometimes it is, but it is not negative or dark or bad. It is meant to spur us to overcome our fears, step into our power, and take charge of our spiritual paths, which is difficult to do if nothing in our lives ever challenges us.

Wicca Is a Magical System

Last, but not least, Wicca is a magical system. There is more than one kind of magic. There is everyday magic, where you do spell work for things like finding a new job or protecting your home. Wiccans make use of this type of magic all the time. But there is also the kind of magic that you use to manifest your own personal power and divinity. In essence, it's working your will to find your purpose in life and align with your higher self. We'll talk more about the will in chapter 2 and magic in chapter 11, but for now, the thing to know is that Wicca is a framework in which to work these two types of magic.

As you can see, there are a lot of interpretations of Wicca. Now that you have made it through the philosophical stuff and you know something about what Wicca is (or what others think it is), you're ready to explore what Wiccans actually believe in chapter 2. But there is one important thing to take from this chapter before you move on: If you choose to walk this path, your Wiccan experience can be pagan, experiential, shamanistic, mystical, magical, or all or none of the above, but the one thing it certainly will be is your own.

Wicca, from any angle, is a path of empowerment and personal growth. Like many things in life, Wicca is what you make of it. The joy—and the challenge—is discovering what it will make of you.

2

Some Basic Wiccan Principles and Ethics

ONE OF MY TEACHERS has commented frequently that Wicca is a religion with a lot of theology (study of the nature of deity) and no dogma (rules imposed by religious leaders). Many people become Wiccans because they're independent souls who don't want to be told what to think or believe. Wicca offers fertile ground and a lot of space for spiritual creativity and independence. Although the Wiccan community is very diverse and is becoming more so all the time, there are a few common principles that most Wiccans share. This chapter will cover seven of these common principles and also a basic Wiccan code of ethics.

Before we dig in, however, here is a list of things that Wiccans do *not* do or believe. It may seem ridiculous that I included some of these, but all of them are here because some Wiccan, at some time, has had to explain to someone that they're not true. So, for the record, Wicca is not:

SATANIC OR ANTI-CHRISTIAN. As I stated in the "new old religion" section in chapter 1, Wicca is not the same thing as Satanic witchcraft. Wiccans do not believe in Satan. Satan is part of the Christian religion, and Satanism is a Christian heresy. Contrary to Hollywood notions, Wiccans do not perform animal or human sacrifice or pervert the Catholic mass. Wiccans do not hate Christians, or try to harm them or their faith. They do, however, wish Christians would stop knocking on their doors and leaving leaflets on their front steps in an effort to convert them. Which leads me to . . .

PROSELYTIZING. Wiccans do not try to convert others to Wicca. Wiccans do not troll the high schools for vulnerable teens to brainwash into secret cults. Wiccans do not go door-to-door trying to convince others that their religion is the right religion. Wiccans know that people in cultures from all over the world, throughout human history—including Christians, Muslims, Jews, Ba'hai, Buddhists, pagans, and others—have been killed for their religious beliefs or forced to adopt someone else's faith, and many Wiccans see proselytizing as a continuation of this bullying and coercion. Wiccans know that there is more than one path to God, and that everyone must find his or her own spirituality (or not, if they choose). Wiccans believe that if people are meant to walk the Wiccan path, they will find it without someone proselytizing to them. Wiccans also know that those who do find the path on their own value it more than they would if they had been "convinced" to become Wiccan.

DUALISTIC. As you'll see in Wiccan Principle 1, below, Wicca incorporates a lot of dual and polarity symbolism. However, although some religions see dualities as antagonistic, like God and Satan, for example, Wiccans see them as opposite partners, or two parts of a whole. That whole "black and white," "absolute right and absolute wrong" mindset has no place in Wicca. Wiccans see many shades of gray. This does not mean that Wiccans have no ethics! See the ethics section toward the end of this chapter for more about that.

EXCLUSIVE. There is nothing in Wicca that says you can't practice more than one religion or worship more than one god or set of gods.

A WAY TO GET POWER OVER OTHERS. Wicca is a way to build your own power. Isn't that more important?

ONLY ABOUT MAGIC. If you are exploring Wicca only so you can learn magic, don't waste your time. Wicca is a religion, and you don't need it to do magic. Magic exists outside of religion. Wicca provides one of many paths to magical practice, but magic is not its central theme. Some Wiccans don't do magic at all.

AN EDGY TREND WITH GREAT CLOTHES. Black vinyl pants and matching lipstick, a pentagram nose ring, a vaguely threatening tattoo, and the latest melancholic, angst-ridden rock CD do not make you a Wiccan. Many Wiccans like fun, unusual body decoration (black is slimming, glitter is fun, and tattoos are good conversation starters), but getting into Wicca to make a fashion statement, because it's trendy, or because it's bound to freak out your parents, neighbors, or boss trivializes the religion. And as long as we're talking about fashions and trends, Goth and Wicca aren't the same thing! Wicca is Goth-friendly because it explores and even embraces death and the darker aspects of spirituality, and there are a lot of Goth Wiccans, but you can be Wiccan whether you're wearing Armani, Hot Topic, Salvation Army, or nothing at all.

AN EXCUSE FOR SEXUAL ABUSE. Wicca is not about using sex to manipulate others or about sexually abusing children. Wiccans find these things as abhorrent as anyone else does. Child abuse is not acceptable, and it is not condoned in the Wiccan path. It's true that Wiccans tend to be pretty open about sex (see Wiccan Principle 7), but because they're frank about sexuality, and even celebrate it, most covens will not accept a student under the age of twenty-one. It's not appropriate to include a child or teenager in rituals that may contain sexual symbolism. That said, if someone tries to tell you that sex is expected as payment for Wiccan training, run screaming into the night. That person is a sexual predator, not a Wiccan.

Here is a list of seven basic things that many Wiccans do believe.

Wiccan Principle 1: Deity Becomes a Polarity

Many Wiccans believe that there is a single great divine force, which they call "spirit," "the all," "the divine," or just "deity." It gives life to the universe, and it transcends gender, space, and time. They also believe, as do practitioners of many of the world's religions, that deity in its entirety is too large and abstract for humans to comprehend fully. In the wonderful *Power of Myth* series of interviews that Bill Moyers conducted with Joseph Campbell, the twentieth century's foremost authority on mythology, Campbell sums up this idea: "God is a thought. God is a name. God is an idea. But its reference is to something that transcends all things. The ultimate mystery of being is beyond all categories of thought."[1]

1. Joseph Campbell, *The Power of Myth,* DVD (Apostrophe S Productions, 1988). Distributed most recently by Mystic Fire Video.

Wiccans believe that deity separates (or we separate it) into facets—or aspects—that humans can relate to. The first "division" of deity is into its male and female halves. In the *Power of Myth* interviews, Campbell describes a beautiful representation of this idea: the Mask of Eternity in the Shiva Cave at Elephanta in India. The mask consists of a central face looking forward and one face looking to each side. Campbell explains that the left and right faces of the mask signify the first division of deity and that "Whenever one moves out of the transcendent [deity], one comes into a field of opposites. These . . . come forth as male and female from the two sides."[2] So by splitting into aspects, deity moves into the field of time, which is where humans exist. Campbell continues: "Everything in the field of time is dual. The past and future. Dead and alive, all this; being and nonbeing, is, isn't."[3]

That's pretty heady stuff, but the Wiccan interpretation of the same idea is fairly straightforward. The two main aspects of deity that Wiccans work with—the male and the female—are simply called the God and the Goddess. The Wiccan God and Goddess represent yang and yin, positive and negative, light and dark. Since they are two halves of the same whole, they are separate but never truly apart; they are connected by their polarity. Neither exists without the other. The polarity—the relationship—between the God and the Goddess is a central, sacred dynamic of Wicca.

2. Campbell, *The Power of Myth*. DVD.
3. Ibid.

Wiccan Principle 2: Deity Is Immanent

Wiccans believe that deity, the life force described in Principle 1, is immanent, or inherent in all people and things. It is in the greatest cathedral and the smallest grain of sand. This is not quite the same thing as the animist idea that a cathedral or a grain of sand have consciousness of their own, but rather that there is a sacred force that infuses everything, and that force is deity or a part of deity. Deity is in each of us as well, regardless of our religion. Because deity is immanent in us, each of us is a part of the divine.

Wiccan Principle 3: The Earth Is Divine

Wiccans believe that the earth is a manifestation of deity. It is a tangible piece of the divine, particularly of the Goddess, who gives birth to all things and receives them again in death. Therefore, everywhere on earth is sacred space. Although you may argue that some places are more sacred than others, Wiccans believe that there's a bit of the divine in every corner of the earth, so they focus on attuning and working with earth energies. This means understanding the cycle of the seasons, participating in these cycles through ritual and contact with the earth, and living within the flow of the earth's natural power rather than working against it.

The ultimate religious experience for many people is to transcend the mundane, the earth, and go to some higher place. It can be a "location," like the Christian heaven, or an inner place, like when one finds enlightenment or Nirvana. Although many Wiccans believe that there is a special place that they go to after they die, and many of them believe in an "otherworld" or "underworld," the majority of their practice is centered in the here and now, on planet earth. For example, Wiccan rituals often mimic the seasonal changes, and Wiccans include trees, rocks, and herbs in ritual and magic.

Many Wiccans believe that a significant part of their spiritual path is taking care of the earth, whether it is by everyday actions such as recycling, larger efforts such as work for environmental causes, or any number of things in between. This is not a requirement of Wicca, but many Wiccans do it anyway because it flows naturally from the belief that the earth is divine.

Wiccan Principle 4: Psychic Power

Wiccans believe that psychic abilities exist, that they work, and that each of us is born with our own psychic gifts. If each of us is infused with the same divine force, and the earth and everything around us are too, we ought to be able to tap into that force to get information and do things beyond the realms of the five senses. We know that many things we encounter in nature occur in patterns, like the shapes of spiral nautilus shells and the patterns of leaves and branches on many trees, the geometry of which are related to the Golden Proportion. (The Greeks, among others, made great use of sacred geometry and the Golden Proportion in building their temples—talk about working in concert with nature!) Wiccans believe that in addition to these well-documented natural phenomena, there are other, less scientifically verifiable patterns in nature and in the spiritual realms, and they work at understanding and using those patterns. Psychic ability is simply a sensitivity to and awareness of those patterns.

Psychic abilities help Wiccans with many things, like honing their intuition, divination (reading astrological charts or tarot cards, for example), and sensing things that science can't explain yet, like the spirits of the dead or the presence of the gods. Like many other talents, psychic abilities can be sharpened, and Wicca can help us harness these gifts. One of the most obvious but important ways in which Wicca does this is simply by teaching us that psychic abilities are real. After all, it's hard to use something that you don't believe exists. Wiccans also strengthen their psychic abilities through practice. They do meditation, magic, divination, and ritual, all of which require them to flex their psychic muscles. I'll go into some of those practices in more depth in the upcoming chapters.

Wiccan Principle 5: Magic

Wiccans believe that magic is real, that it works, and that they can use it to better their lives and help them on their spiritual journeys. By magic, I don't mean pulling rabbits out of hats, turning your younger brother into a toad, or hexing your ex-girlfriend. I mean something closer to the definition of magic given by the famous (and infamous) twentieth-century magician Aleister Crowley in his equally famous book *Magick in Theory and Practice*. Magic (or magick, to Crowley) is "the science and art of causing change to occur in conformance with will."[4]

Magic, like psychic ability, depends on knowledge of the patterns of the cosmos. But where using psychic ability means attuning to and understanding those patterns, magic means bending or working with them to bring about desired change. The philosophy of magic goes back again to the idea that everything is infused with the divine. If all things contain some divine energy, we can tap into that energy to affect things that seem—to the regular five senses, anyway—to have no connection to us. This idea is summed up neatly in the introduction to *Magick in Theory and Practice*, which opens with the following quote from *The Goetia of the Lemegeton of King Solomon*, a magical grimoire, or spellbook:

> Magic is the highest, most absolute, and most divine knowledge of natural philosophy, advanced in its works and wonderful operations by a right understanding of the inward and occult virtue of things, so that true agents being applied to proper patients, strange and admirable effects will thereby be produced. Whence magicians are profound and diligent searchers into nature; they, because of their skill, know how to anticipate an effect, which to the vulgar shall seem to be a miracle.[5]

4. Aleister Crowley, *Magick in Theory and Practice* (New York: Magickal Childe Publishing, 1990), p. xii.
5. Ibid., p. ix.

As with psychic ability, one of the ways in which Wicca helps people develop magical abilities is simply by allowing them to believe that magic is possible. Another way is by teaching us that each of us must find our own path and moral compass—our magical will. Magic is a tool for empowerment and personal growth. True, Wiccans use magic all the time for mundane things, like healing. But its ultimate purpose transcends the mundane.

Wiccan Principle 6: Reincarnation

Although most Wiccans will tell you that they believe in reincarnation—the soul returning to the earth again in a new body or form after death—their views vary widely on what that means. Some simply believe that our souls are reborn into new bodies, and others think that our essence "recycles" after our bodies die and becomes cosmic energy. Some even believe that we all share one soul, and that this soul experiences the many possibilities of life by inhabiting all of our bodies at the same time.

Gerald Gardner, the "grandfather" of Wicca whom I mentioned in chapter 1, believed strongly in reincarnation. Part of the reason he was accused of being a publicity hound in his day was that he was trying to drum up interest in Wicca so the Craft wouldn't die out and he'd have a Wiccan family to be reborn into. This focus on reincarnation stems in part from what I called Wiccan Principle 3; that the earth is divine. As we've already seen, Wiccan practice is earth-focused;

here-and-now-focused. It's natural, then, that Wiccans would believe that death is not the end of their existence, and that they're going to be back again in some form, some day.

Wiccan Principle 7: Sex Is Sacred

In Wicca, sex, the physical joining of two people, is a sacred act, one that brings joy and wonder, not shame and guilt. Sex is treasured and revered. Sexuality is considered a gift from the gods, a pleasure and responsibility that comes with a physical body, and a manifestation of the polarity of the God and Goddess and the fertility of the earth.

There is a lot of sexual symbolism in Wicca. The sabbats—the Wiccan holidays—include stories of the union of the God and Goddess. The chalice and athame (ritual knife) on the Wiccan altar represent female and male reproductive organs, among other things. And the focus in Wicca on the cycles of nature emphasizes fertility of both the earth and its people.

Does the prevalence of God-and-Goddess and fertility symbolism mean that gay sex is taboo in Wicca, since gay sex doesn't involve both a female and a male? Absolutely not! Polarity is expressed whenever two consenting adults come together to make love, and gay sex is as much about enjoying our earthy humanity as heterosexual sex is.

Does holding sex sacred mean that Wiccans have ceremonial orgies? That's not the point of sacred sex in Wicca. Understanding the spiritual side of sex frees some people from society's tight constraints about sex, so they may be more likely to experiment with multiple partners (which is hardly an orgy). But the idea that sex is sacred also means that it should be treated with reverence, which gives Wiccans a reason to approach sexual relationships with greater care and respect than they might if they viewed sex as simply mundane. An eighty-something-year-old medicine woman from central Mexico that I know puts it this way: "You are sacred. Your body is sacred. Your vagina is sacred. Your penis is sacred. You don't put anything that isn't sacred in your sacred body. And you don't put your sacred body into anything that isn't sacred." I can't think of a better way to say it than that.

If you are uncomfortable with the idea of sex as sacred or of sexual symbolism, Wicca probably is not the path for you. That may sound harsh, especially in the United States, where we're taught that we can be anything that we want to be. But the truth is that Wicca challenges us. It is not meant to be comfortable or static. We do not change when we're not challenged to do so, and a great deal of Wicca is about change and the personal power that comes from embracing it. The idea that sex is sacred is only one of the many ways that Wicca might challenge some commonly accepted social norms.

Ethics and Empowerment

As you may have gathered, Wiccans are pretty independent folk. It should not surprise you, then, that there is no centralized authority that determines Wiccan ethics. Ethics are essentially principles of good conduct; rules about proper behavior. The ethics or morals of most religions stem from the culture in which the religion developed, the religious institutions (if any) that evolved within the religion, and the religion's sacred books and teachings. Christianity, for example, has its Ten Commandments, which the Bible tells us came to humanity from God by way of Moses.

In Wicca, however, there are no "thou shalt's." There is no book, religious figure, or burning bush to tell Wiccans what is ethical and what is not and what will happen to them if they screw up. One of the empowering—but terrifying—things about Wicca is that a Wiccan has to determine what ethics to follow for him- or herself.

Does this mean that Wicca is a free-for-all, where people do whatever they want, whenever they want, to whomever they want with no consequences or restrictions? Does it mean that there are no Wiccan guidelines for ethical behavior at all? No, and the following section tells you all about this.

The Wiccan Rede

Although there is nobody to tell them that they have to, many Wiccans follow a principle of ethics called the Wiccan Rede, which states: "An it harm none, do as you will." It's a bit like a Wiccan "Golden Rule."

At first glance, the Rede seems to be saying, "Do whatever you want, but don't harm anybody or anything." This is great, in principle; think before you act, don't hex that annoying telemarketer, and try to walk through this world doing as little damage as possible. But many people who interpret the Rede that way get hung up on the word "harm." Visit the archives of any Wiccan email list and you're bound to find a discussion of the Rede where the participants pick the word to death, trying to define exactly just what constitutes harm. This conversation can, and almost always does, go to ridiculous places: "Did I harm someone when I got my new job because it meant that he or she didn't get it?" "Did I harm my friend when I didn't tell her about the half-off sale at Victoria's Secret?" "Did I cause harm when I squashed that big spider in my bathtub?"

Although this can be an interesting philosophical exercise, it misses the point. After all, if you want to go this far, everything, by its mere existence, hurts something else. Trying not to harm anything to the point of asceticism—self-denial as a measure of one's spirituality—defeats the point of Wicca, which celebrates life instead of trying to control it. In fact, "harm none" also means that you should not harm yourself either, and imposing this rigid morality muzzle on your life is hardly a healthy thing to do. If you're not harming anyone else, but you're not living your life either, you're still not living the Rede. The good news is that the important part of the Rede—the true power—is not the word "harm." It is the word "will."

The "Want" and the "Will"

Your "want" is, well, what you want. You want a new car or a date with Cameron Diaz or a pint of Ben and Jerry's. Want is about earthly things, both trivial and important. Your will, however, is the force that drives you to your ultimate spiritual goal. It transcends want. It's the thing that Joseph Campbell is referring to when he says, "Follow your bliss." Campbell's "bliss" is the inner knowing that puts you on the life path that will lead you to your highest mundane and spiritual purpose. In the print version of *The Power of Myth*, he states:

> If you do follow your bliss, you put yourself on a kind of track that has been there all the while, waiting for you, and the life that you ought to be living is the one you are living. When you can see that, you begin to meet people who are in the field of your bliss, and they open the doors to you. I say, follow your bliss and don't be afraid, and doors will open where you didn't know they were going to be.[6]

The same could be said for following, or doing, your will. As you can see, this is a much bigger deal than "do what you want."

The Rede, with its emphasis on will, is challenging you to act according to your highest purpose; to infuse your spirituality, whatever it is, throughout your entire life. It's telling you to act out of that spiritual place when you make decisions. When you act in accordance with your true will, you are in harmony with deity. The focus of the Rede is really on you, your life, and your choices; not on someone you may or may not harm by your actions. It's all about personal respon-

6. Joseph Campbell, *The Power of Myth* (New York: Doubleday, 1988), p. 120.

sibility and self-knowledge, which is both scary and freeing because you are accountable for yourself. The Rede is about both ethics and empowerment.

The Threefold Law

Since there are no morality police in Wicca, there is nobody to determine if Wiccans have done something right or wrong other than they themselves, and there is no cosmic time-out place they will be sent to if they have been misbehaving. This doesn't mean they're off the hook, though.

Many Wiccans believe in the "Threefold Law." The Threefold Law essentially says that whatever you put out into the world will come back to you three times. As with the word harm in the Rede, you can get hung up on "threefold" and argue about whether your deeds come back three separate times or one time, three times as strong, but that isn't the point. The point is simply "like attracts like." If you put positive energy out into the universe, living by your own set of ethics, trying to do "good" for yourself and others, you're likely to receive that kind of energy in return. If you put negative energy out, you'll get that back too. The difference is that when the good stuff comes back, it makes things in your life flow smoothly, and when the negative stuff comes back, it tends to sneak up on you and whack you on the head.

This is not to say that there is a cosmic energy bank somewhere in which you deposit good or bad deeds and someone monitors your account to make sure that your withdrawals reflect what you put in. The universe just doesn't work that way. It doesn't keep scorecards, so don't take the Law literally and expect an immediate reward or head-whacking for whatever you do. You also have no control of *how* it comes back to you. Letting someone merge in front of you on a crowded highway doesn't mean that someone will do the same for you later.

The Rede and the Threefold Law Together

When you put the Law and the Rede together, you see that if you are working your true will, if you are in sync with the universe and the divine, the positive energy you generate ripples out and affects everything around you, and it's a beacon for other positive energy to be attracted to you. This is the place where Wiccans strive to be.

Taking personal responsibility is a major part of Wiccan practice. If Wiccans who adhere to the Rede and the Law screw up or do something nasty to someone, they know that they will attract that energy back in its own place and time. In addition, when you hurt others, you are also hurting yourself, even if it is only indirectly through the negative energy you will attract. Hurting others marks you, and the energy signature sticks to you like flypaper. Even knowing this, sometimes Wiccans will take a risk and choose to do something that is ethically "iffy" because they believe that ultimately it's for the greater good. In that case, they take responsibility for the results, and they know that whatever they receive back, positive or negative, is partially their own doing. The important thing is that they are the arbiters of their own ethics; they have the responsibility and the power to choose their actions based on their own ideals rather than on rules imposed by someone else. This can be heavy stuff, but like I said earlier, Wicca is not about being comfortable all the time. It is about directing the course of your own life, and that can put you on shaky turf from time to time.

In the next chapters we're going to explore some of the foundation practices of Wicca, including energy work, visualization, trance work, meditation, and pathworking. If you are considering trying your hand at these skills and doing the exercises in the upcoming chapters, this would be a good time to start a journal to record your experiences. A journal can help you keep track of your progress and provide a record of the insights you've gained along the way.

3

Fundamental Wiccan Tools:

Energy, Visualization, Grounding, and Shielding

If you've read this far (instead of just skipping to this page), you've taken in a lot of philosophical stuff about what Wicca is and what Wiccans believe. Understanding that information is essential to understanding Wicca, but it's also important to remember that Wicca is a hands-on religion. Wiccans don't just follow their religion; they explore it, participate in it, live it.

Actively participating in Wicca requires a few basic tools, or skills. The most fundamental tool you have as a Wiccan—or just as a person, for that matter—is your mind. This chapter and the next will focus on the mind in order to lay the groundwork for you to learn about ritual and magic. A lot of Wiccan practice is centered around training your mind and using it in new ways. Perhaps the most essential, basic mental practices in Wicca are visualization, grounding, and shielding. Before you dive into those, however, it's important to understand a little bit about energy.

What Is Energy?

All life is infused with energy. As Obi Wan Kenobi says of the "Force" in the 1977 movie *Star Wars*, "It's an energy field created by all living things. It surrounds us and penetrates us. It binds the galaxy together." He could be describing what Wiccans call "energy" just as easily. For some Wiccans, energy and what I've been calling deity are the same thing: the life force. For others, deity is sentient and energy is not. Still others think that energy emanates from deity, or comes from the Goddess. In several of his books, Scott Cunningham, a famous Wiccan author, stated that he felt there were three types of energy, which he called power. The first is personal power, the energy that resides and is generated by your own body. The second is divine power, the energy that comes from the gods. The third is earth power, the energy that infuses and is generated by the earth. This is a useful way to think about energy in Wicca, as long as you remember that ultimately all three types of energy are the same thing, despite the fact that they "reside" and are generated from different sources. Whichever viewpoint they subscribe to, most Wiccans believe that everything contains some sort of energy.

Energy is important in Wicca. Wiccans hone their ability to feel and "read" it in order to understand the cycles of nature better, to tune in to their surroundings, and to get psychic information. Wiccans also believe that they can bend and use energy to bring about change, which is what magic is all about.

As with so many things in Wicca, you must either believe that energy exists in all things or at least have an open mind about it if you really want to learn to feel and use it. It's true that you might feel energy "by accident," whether you believe in it or not. If you've ever walked into a party and felt the vibe of the group, or stood in a very old church and sensed the gentle hum of the power that has collected there during years of worship, you've felt energy. It's a heck of a lot easier if you relax, turn off your inner Mr. Spock, and allow yourself to feel it. Here are some basic exercises to get you started.

exercise 1: hand to hand

This is a tried-and-true "first energy experience" technique. Nearly every Wiccan I know has used this trick at least once. Find a place where you can sit quietly and undisturbed for a while. It can be on the floor, in a chair, outside, or whatever is comfortable for you. It's important that you be able to relax. Sit up straight if you can do so while you are still relaxed. I've found that my ability to do energy work is enhanced when my spine is straight. Sitting up straight may or may not work for you, so experiment with your posture.

Once you're comfy, rub your hands together gently for several seconds until you feel warmth between them. Then hold your hands together in front of you as if you were a child saying a bedtime prayer, and slowly move them apart a few inches. As you move them apart, see if you can feel the energy that you just raised zip between your palms or fingers (and I'm talking energy here, not warmth!). For some people the energy feels, or even looks, a bit like you are playing cat's cradle with string between your hands. Don't expect a lightning strike here; this energy is subtle and tingly. I tend to feel it emanating from the center of my palms; others feel it from their fingers.

Next try moving your hands gently and slowly back together. As you do this, see if you can feel any resistance between your hands. For some people, this feels like the push that happens when you put the wrong ends of two magnets together and they repel each other. Don't be discouraged if you don't feel anything the first time you try this. If you practice this exercise, you will feel it eventually.

A variation on this technique is to work with a partner. Sit facing your partner, rub your own hands together like you did when you were alone, and have your partner do the same. Then touch your hands to your partner's as if you were both pushing opposite sides of a door or playing patty-cake. Try pulling your hands away from each other slowly and see if you can feel the energy between you. Then try to feel the resistance as you push your hands back up to your partner's.

Some Wiccans believe that they have a "receptive" and an "active" hand. The receptive hand is better at feeling energy, and the active hand is better at directing it. Most Wiccans who believe this say that their dominant hand is the active one, so if you are right-handed, it would be best to try this energy-feeling exercise with your left. Personally, I've never felt that one of my hands is receptive and one active—they both work for both things—but there are people in my coven who swear by the "receptive hand" theory. This is another one of those points that you can experiment with to find which way works best for you. Maybe your feet are better than either of your hands!

exercise 2: stones and sticks

Once you have felt the energy in your hands, try to feel energy in a crystal or stone. Hint: crystals are natural batteries, so their energy tends to be easy to feel. Sit comfortably, relax, and pick up the stone or crystal in your hand. Hold it gently, and see what you feel. You may not feel anything with your hand at all, but rather "feel" the sensation in your head. You may get a mental image instead of a physical sensation. Or you may just feel the crystal zinging in your palm. Try a variety of different stones. Is their energy different? If so, how? Are some easier to sense than others? If you find a particular stone that "sings" to you, you may want to keep it for magical work.

Next, see if you can feel the energy in plants or trees. Again, find a place where you can relax and work undisturbed, this time outside. Sit or stand near a plant or tree, and hold your hands a couple of inches away from it. Yes, you may feel silly doing this. Your neighbors will think you are weird if they see you doing it in your yard. So what? It's all in the name of experimentation and spiritual growth, right? Shut your eyes, and try to feel the difference in the energy as you move your hands slowly toward the plant. You should not need to touch the plant to feel its energy "signature," but touch it if you can't feel anything without doing so. This might be easier with a smaller plant than a tree. Trees are big, and they have wonderful, strong energy signatures, but they're not as zippy, for lack of a better word, as, for example, the oregano plant in your garden. If the tree is a bass, the herb is a soprano.

When you have felt the energy of stones and plants, try working with household objects. They have energy signatures too. Try to feel the energy of a block of wood or a plastic toy. The vibe may not be as strong as it is with plants and crystals, but it should still be there. Wiccans who become adept at feeling energy in inanimate objects often try their hands at psychometry. Psychometry is the ability to touch something and get information about its past from its vibration; for example, picking up an old photograph and learning something about the people pictured. Don't feel that you are not a good Wiccan if you can't do full-blown psychometry, though. Many, many Wiccans can't do it either! The important thing is to keep practicing and trying to feel energy.

Energy Follows Thought: Visualization

Once you've felt energy, you can begin to learn how to work with it to do ritual, become more familiar with deity, work magic, and make positive changes in your life. The first step in doing this is to learn about visualization. Wiccans use visualization constantly in magic and energy work. In Wicca, visualization means creating a picture in your mind's eye of what you want to happen. There is a magical idea that "energy follows thought." What that means is that if you create and see something in your mind, that image attracts energy, and whatever you're picturing begins to become a reality.

This is not the same as the crazy "new age" idea that if we all got together and held hands and visualized world peace, the armies of the world would lay down their weapons, all borders would vanish, and everyone would get along. Visualization is more like using affirmations. Affirmations are positive statements that you repeat over and over to yourself to impress them on your subconscious—that deep, mysterious part of your brain that operates below the level of your conscious mind. If you can imprint a concept on your subconscious mind, the subconscious works to make the idea a reality. Unlike your conscious mind, which is tied more closely to your everyday life and probably has a healthy dose of skepticism, your subconscious mind believes everything it's told. It's very literal. When you look in the mirror and say, "I'm going to lose five pounds," your subconscious mind says, "I'm going to lose five pounds." Your conscious mind says, "It'll only work if I cut out the Ho Hos." It's not that the conscious doesn't believe you, but rather that it doesn't accept your statement as truth without question. The subconscious has no such analytical barriers.

But the subconscious—enigmatic thing that it is—works better with pictures than it does with words. So if you can learn to visualize what you want to happen, it will be easier for your mind to grasp what you're aiming for than if you just say it out loud. When you form an image in your mind—even your conscious mind—it begins to become a reality for you. The more often you visualize something, the more real it becomes in your mind. And the more real it becomes in your mind, the more real it is elsewhere too.

Here are some tricks you can try to improve your ability to visualize. When you're trying these, it helps to start in a quiet place where you can work undisturbed, as you did with the energy-sensing exercises. Over time, you'll get better and better at visualizing until you can do it anywhere, even amidst distractions. But when you are just starting to hone this skill, it's better to give yourself some peace and quiet.

---

exercise 3: everyday things

Pick up a smallish object that you see every day, such as your alarm clock, a shoe, your car keys, or a can opener. Spend five minutes examining the item. Turn it over in your hands.

Feel it. Smell it (even if it's your shoe). Notice its weight, its tiny details. Once you've examined the object, put it down, close your eyes, and visualize it. Picture it as a whole, and also picture all of the details you found. See if you can re-create the item in your mind. Once you have done this, hold the picture in your mind for several seconds or as long as you can. When you can no longer hold on to the image, open your eyes. Try this exercise several times with the object in front of you. Then practice doing it without looking at the object first. Pick up the object afterward and see if there are any details you missed.

Once you've had success working with a household object, try working with a houseplant. The trick with this is that the plant will change slightly every day. See if you can notice the differences from day to day, and shift yesterday's picture to reflect today's changes. Then try it with a pet or a friend's face. It's important to be able to visualize your loved ones if you think you might want to do healing magic for them in the future, and it's also great practice.

exercise 4: the birthday party game

We call this exercise the Birthday Party Game because we always played it at birthday parties when we were kids. You may have too.

Ask a friend to gather about ten small household objects and lay them on a table in front of you. Ask him or her to time you as you look at the objects for thirty seconds, and then to cover up the objects with a blanket. During your thirty seconds, examine the objects as carefully as you can. Once they are covered up, see if you can remember what and where all of them were, and picture them in your mind. Take another thirty-second look if necessary. Once you know the items and their layout, have your friend rearrange them, and try again. The point is not to memorize the objects as you would for a test; it's to be able to conjure the image of the pile of objects in your mind.

exercise 5: location, location, location

Sit in a chair in your living room, close your eyes, and visualize the room. Try to see as much detail as you can in your mind. Open your eyes, and notice what you missed. Close them again and see if you can enhance your mental picture with the new details. When you're good at visualizing one room, move to another room, or try this at work, on the bus, or in the grocery aisle—anyplace where you can close your eyes for a moment without bumping into someone or causing a car accident.

Don't stop practicing visualization, even after you become proficient. Keeping your visualization skills honed is like working out at the gym; you have to keep doing it to maintain the highest level of ability. Actually, practicing at the gym when you're working on a repetitive, boring cardio machine isn't a bad idea. Practice recalling details about the people and things around you instead of watching TV or surfing the Internet. Whether you do it at the gym or not, however, if you begin doing ritual and energy work, you're going to get lots of practice.

Two Vital Skills: Grounding and Shielding

Before you explore energy work further, it's important that you put your newly polished visualization skills to work to help you learn two core energy techniques: grounding and shielding. These techniques will allow you to have more control in your energy work by giving you ways to get rid of excess energy and protect yourself from unwanted energy.

Grounding

Perhaps the most vital skill a Wiccan can learn is called "grounding," or "grounding and centering." The earth is one of our greatest sources of energy. Since it is alive, it radiates energy all the time. It can also store and neutralize energy. When Wiccans do magic, they usually do not use their personal body energy (what Cunningham called "personal power") because they need that for everyday life. Instead, they draw energy from the earth (earth power) through their bodies. Likewise, when Wiccans have too much energy, such as when they haven't been able to use all the energy they raised in a powerful ritual, or when they've picked up "bad" energy in an argument, they return the excess energy to the earth. This is what grounding is. Think of how we ground electrical outlets, and you've got the idea.

Many Wiccans begin every ritual or magical act by grounding. They cast off unwanted "vibes" from their day, like the tension left over from a stressful meeting at work or road rage from nasty traffic. By grounding, they also connect to mother earth, from whom the energy for the ritual will come. If you are grounding in order to "shake off" your day before ritual, don't worry about sending "negative" or "bad" energy into the earth. Like I said, the earth neutralizes energy. Anything you send to it will be transformed and will manifest in other ways.

It is vital to be able to ground before you move on to raising and working with energy. There is an old, old rule in magic that you should never call up anything that you don't know how to banish. The magician who came up with that was referring to spirits, demons, or other scary-but-useful entities from the medieval magical grimoires, but when I say it here, I mean that before you raise energy, you should know how to get rid of it. If you carry it around in your body, or allow it to zip around your home without direction or purpose, it can have all sorts of weird effects, not the least of which is that you will feel out of whack until it dissipates or you manage to ground it out.

How do you know when you have too much energy, need to ground, or both? You may feel lightheaded, dizzy, or "out of it." You may feel a little queasy. You may feel wound up, nervous, or angry. Some people even feel a little bit drunk. None of these conditions are suitable for ritual or magic, but you don't have to reserve grounding for Wiccan or magical purposes. You can ground anytime you need to, for any reason. I've even done it before job interviews.

There are as many ways to ground as there are Wiccans. The one that I teach my students follows. We do this technique as a meditation, so it is a bit repetitive. It was designed that way on purpose because repetition helps you relax, and when you're relaxed, it's easier to visualize and imprint images on your subconscious. You may wish to read this exercise into a tape recorder and play it back for yourself when you practice. I've put pauses in the meditation in case you wish to record it. "Pause" means to pause the reading, not the activity.

exercise 6: the taproot

As you did with the previous exercises, find a quiet place where you can work undisturbed. You do not have to be outside, but you should be able to visualize or sense the earth beneath you. Sit comfortably and relax. Take a few deep breaths. When you are calm and relaxed, imagine that there is a thick, golden, glowing taproot that extends from the base of your spine all the way down into the center of the earth. It is vibrant, and it draws its energy from the earth's molten core. See it and feel it in your mind as strongly as you can. Know that it connects you to the earth, the Mother Goddess, and the web of life. Pause.

When you can see the taproot in your mind's eye and you "know" its reality within you, gently draw warm energy up from the earth through it. Feel and/or see the energy flow up the taproot to the base of your spine. Pause. Imagine that the energy branches from the top of the taproot, and some of it flows down each of your legs and into each foot. Feel the energy moving gently into your legs and feet. Pause. Then imagine that the energy runs from the taproot all the way up your spine. Feel the energy move gently up your spine. Pause. Then imagine that the energy splits from the top of the spine and runs down each arm and into your hands. Feel the energy move gently down your arms and into your hands. Pause. Finally, imagine that the energy moves from the top of your spine to the top of your head. Feel your whole body full of glowing earth energy. Know that you are connected to the earth and the web of all life. Pause.

Once you have visualized the energy filling your body, imagine gently pushing the excess energy out of your head, arms, legs, and spine back down into the taproot, and from there into the earth. Keep your body energy, but see any energy that you do not want flowing down through the taproot and neutralizing in the earth. Feel it leave your body. *You are not drained because you are not pushing out your own energy.*

It is helpful for some people to "collect" the energy at the top of the taproot before pushing it out, while others like to push it down from all parts of the body at the same time. Whichever way is easiest for you is the best way.

If you do this exercise enough times, the taproot will become real. I knew that the meditation was working with my students when I took them to a big, open public ritual, and the ritual leader asked everyone to ground beforehand by extending a root into the earth. We were standing in a circle with a lot of other people, and the moment the leader said that, I could feel the "taproots" of all of my students shoot into the ground one after the other around the circle. It was a little bit like dominoes falling in a row. I knew that some of the other ritual participants who were not in our group could feel it too by the funny looks they gave us.

Whenever you need to ground, you can push excess energy out of your body through your taproot. Practice taking up and returning energy to the earth many times before you attempt to do any additional energy or spell work. By repeating the exercise, you are "burning" the image of the taproot into your mind and making it more and more real to your subconscious.

As I said, there are lots of other ways to ground too. If the taproot idea doesn't work for you, try something else. Here's a quick-and-dirty list of ideas. Experiment with these, or find another that makes sense and works well for you.

Quick Grounding Techniques and Visualizations

BREATHING. Breathe slowly and deeply, and imagine pushing excess energy out of your body with each exhalation. Don't draw in extra energy with the inhalation; just draw in air. Remember to breathe slowly. Breathing in and out quickly helps you raise energy rather than get rid of it.

SHAKING HANDS. Visualize pushing the excess energy into your hands, then shake it out of your hands as if you were shaking water off of them. Just be careful not to aim at anyone or "hit" others by accident. You can make someone very queasy this way.

TREE GROUNDING. As with shaking hands, visualize pushing the excess energy into your hands. Touch the trunk of a tree, and imagine the excess energy flowing from your hands into the tree, down the trunk, out the roots, and into the earth. I tried this once when I was at an outdoor audition for my vocal group, and it saved my bacon. I found out at the last minute that I would have to be the soloist instead of just a backup singer. I was scared to death, so I gave all of my jitters to a very obliging oak tree in the park. As I touched its trunk, I could feel the fear flow out of my stomach, through my arms, and into the tree and earth. I'm sure my performance would have been a warbling mess if I hadn't grounded first.

STONES. You can use the tree grounding technique with a stone. We keep a large hunk of jet that I got from a gem and mineral show in a drawer in our altar so people can pull it out and ground with it if they need to. They may push energy into the stone with their hands, or even put the stone up to their foreheads and let the energy run into the rock from their "third eye"—the energy center in the center of the forehead, between the brows. Your stone doesn't have to be large, though. It can be pocket-sized so you can carry it with you anywhere. I have a small piece of jet in my purse for that reason. Folklore has it that black stones like jet or obsidian work best for grounding, but I've had good luck with hematite too. Others swear that any good solid rock that they find in the woods or by a stream will do. Once you have grounded yourself with the rock, you can ground the rock and "empty" it of whatever you've put into it by placing it in running water, in a bowl of salt, or simply on the ground. This isn't always necessary, but as you saw from the energy-feeling exercises earlier, some rocks really retain energy (crystals, in particular, are like rechargeable batteries), and if you're going to use the same rock to ground with later, it may be a good idea to "empty" it. There are lots of excellent books about the properties of rocks, and many of them list which rocks are good for grounding. See the suggested reading list for more information.

RUNNING WATER. Sitting by or getting into running water is another excellent grounding technique. Stand in the shower and visualize excess energy running off of you with the water. If you have the luxury of living near a clean stream or river, or even by the ocean, swimming in flowing water is a great alternative. One word of caution: If you have so much energy that you're feeling loopy or dizzy, keep someone nearby to monitor you if you're going to ground in water. You don't want to slip in the shower and crack your head or get sucked into the undertow, because then you would need a different type of grounding altogether.

EATING. Eating can bring you back to earth quickly. It's hard to stay dizzy or heady when your stomach is full. If you're eating to ground, slowly eat a small portion of something solid, preferably without a lot of sugar or caffeine in it. Sugar and caffeine will give you the shakes. A slice of cheese, salami, or good, heavy bread will do. You won't need much food to ground, and overeating when you're grounding can make your stomach uncomfortable. Many Wiccan rituals include a small ceremonial meal or snack to help participants ground.

THE DIRECT ROUTE. Perhaps the easiest, no-props way to ground is to get down on your hands and knees and press your forehead into the floor or ground. Imagine the excess energy flowing from your forehead into the earth. I attended a ritual at a big pagan festival where the ritual leaders provided a large, flat stone for people to kneel in front of and lay their foreheads on. Public rituals can be pretty heady, if only because there are so many people there, and this was a great solution to the problem of people wandering away from the ritual site without grounding.

Shielding

Like grounding, it is important to understand shielding before you begin more advanced energy work. "Shielding" is essentially creating an energy field around you that helps you control what energies you pick up from the world around you and what energies you give off. To continue with my *Star Wars* comparisons, it's like the force field around the Death Star—an invisible protection that you can take down or put up at will. You can create a shield that keeps everything out or a semi-permeable one that only filters out negative stuff like a sieve and lets the rest through.

Most people have natural shields that pop into place when they're uncomfortable or scared. To protect yourself, your mind already may have built a "not if you were the last man (or woman) on earth" shield that you unconsciously put up when some creepy person sits next to you during happy hour. Or maybe you've got a "please, please don't notice me" shield for when you didn't prepare for your class or business meeting and you don't want your teacher or boss to ask you questions about the material. (Word to the wise: Don't use the "don't notice me" shield when you're driving. You're more likely to get home in one piece if the other drivers can see you.) These are more traditional "barrier" shields, but you may also already have a shield that gives off a specific kind of energy that you want to project, such as the "I'm strong and powerful, and I could take Jet Li in a fight with one arm tied behind my back, so don't mess with me" shield for when you are walking down a dark street alone.

Why do you need a shield? When Wiccans work with energy and try to improve their psychic skills, they naturally become more sensitive to their environment, and shielding helps them filter out ambient energetic "noise." You probably don't want to pick up the vibes of everyone around you in a crowded restaurant, for example, or a shopping mall the day after Thanksgiving. If you're psychically sensitive, it's easy to get overwhelmed in noisy public places. Sometimes, too, we have to deal with "toxic" people at work or elsewhere, and although we can't avoid them, we can shield ourselves to prevent the negative stuff that they exude from sticking to us. Once Wiccans have created shields that strain out that extraneous stuff, they can focus on whatever ritual or spell work they're doing without energetic interruption, and draw in only the energy that they need and want.

When some Wiccan students first hear the word shield, they interpret it as if it were referring to a literal suit of armor, and begin to worry that if they do energy work they will need to protect themselves from evil spirits or black magic. Don't worry—working with earth energy is not going to attract negative energy beasties and malevolent imps to your front door. You'd have to be doing some pretty dark magic to conjure up things like that—if they even exist at all. You also might encounter people who say they use shields to ward off "psychic attack" or negative magic directed at them. Most of the time, this is just plain silly. It's true that you can use a shield to prevent such an attack, but don't go worrying that people are using some secret psychic power to mess with you. Most people either can't or won't carry out a psychic attack against someone else. It's not that easy, and it's not at all common. With the Rede and Threefold Law, any Wiccan would think twice before attempting psychic attack. When someone tells you that they're under psychic attack, take it with a grain of salt. It's certainly not impossible, but more often than not, people create stories like this to ferment a little drama and get some attention.

That said, a shield is still an important tool for a Wiccan to have. Building one is simple.

exercise 7: shielding

First, think of an image that you could use to protect yourself. For example, it's common for Wiccans to imagine their shields as a bubble encircling their bodies. Others imagine that they're wearing a suit of armor or are surrounded by a ring of fire. I have one student who uses a castle with a moat and drawbridge, and a friend who imagines a powerful snake coiled around her (loosely, of course). Choose something that you can picture easily and that you don't think is silly.

Once you have chosen an image, sit comfortably and relax. Ground. Take several deep breaths. Imagine a ball of energy sitting at the top of your taproot. Make it a color that you associate with protection. Visualize the ball of energy until it feels real to you. Then extend the energy to surround your body and take the shape of the image that you've chosen. If you're working with a bubble, you might see the energy as a blue bubble that begins in your body but grows to expand past the bounds of your body and surround you. Use visualization to make the bubble real and solid. Imagine unwanted energies bouncing harmlessly off the surface. Stand up and move around. Your shield should move with you. Practice keeping it up while doing ordinary tasks such as vacuuming or brushing your teeth. Visualize it until it is absolutely real for you.

Practice shielding regularly in a quiet space. When you think you've got it down, try doing it in public and see if people react to you differently. Remember that this shield is purely defensive; it's not meant to project your energy at others. Try using it in several different places and circumstances, and note what feels different about it in each one. And don't just practice putting it up. Take it down too. To do that, simply "suck" the energy back into the ball at the top of your taproot, and ground out any excess energy through the taproot. See how quickly you can put your shield up and take it down. Practice doing this in a crowded place where there are many distractions.

If the bubble image doesn't work for you, here are a few others to try. Remember, though, that the strongest shield will be the one you make up yourself.

- Imagine that you are surrounded by a brick wall. The

wall is impenetrable, but it is light, and it moves with you.

- Imagine that you are surrounded by a ball or ring of fire.
- Imagine that your skin is a shiny, reflective surface that bounces back any energies you don't want.
- Imagine that you are wearing a light but impenetrable cloak and hood.
- Imagine that you are surrounded by protective light in the color of your choice.
- Imagine that you are wearing an energetic haz-mat suit.
- Imagine that you are surrounded by barbed wire. (Only use this one if you don't want anyone to come near you.)
- Imagine that you are surrounded by a wall or ring of clear ice.

---

exercise 8: shielding with a partner

Now that you've got a strong shield, try working with a partner to see if you can feel each others' shields. Sit in chairs or on the floor, facing each other. Start with your shields down. Ask your partner to start with his or her hands far away from you and then slowly move them toward you, stopping when he or she feels your natural shield. This is not the shield that you have created for protection; this is your natural energy field. For some people this field extends several inches out from the body, and for others it's very close to the skin. It will feel like gentle resistance. Once your partner has felt your natural shield, see if you can feel his or hers.

Next, raise your shields. Do not tell each other what images you are using. Pump a fair amount of energy into your shield. Project your energy outward, as if you were protecting yourself, but remember not to project it at your partner like you are attacking. Tell your partner to move his or her hands forward slowly again and tell you when he or she feels your shield. Have him or her describe how it feels. Is it different than your natural shield, or similar? Can he or she guess what image you're using just by feeling the shield? Then switch and try to feel your partner's shield. Try to guess what he or she is visualizing. Ground when you are finished.

Remember to Practice!

I know I've said this already, but it bears repeating: Practice, practice, practice your visualization, grounding, and shielding. When you do these exercises, you are training your mind and preparing it for ritual and magical work, among other things. Burn these skills into your brain so that you're able to do them anywhere, at any time, and even on autopilot. You'll need them to explore trance, meditation, and pathworking, three of a Wiccan's most powerful and versatile practices.

4

Trance, Meditation, and Pathworking

WICCANS USE TRANCE, MEDITATION, and pathworking to train their minds and work with the subconscious to harness their mental powers. There are many reasons a Wiccan might want to use each technique or all three together, including mental exercise, grounding, communicating with the gods, magic, dream work, shamanic journeying, creating an astral temple, healing, and just plain relaxation. We'll talk a little more about some of these later in the chapter.

Both meditation and pathworking involve entering a light trance state and then using visualization to set an image in your mind. The primary difference between the two, for the purposes of this book (you will find different definitions elsewhere), is that when you are doing a pathworking, your visualization usually involves a guided mental journey to a particular place for a particular purpose. A meditation can be much more freeform, and there may or may not be a "journey" involved.

The first step to doing a meditation or pathworking is to relax and allow yourself to enter a light trance state. But first, you need to know how to "trance."

Trance

A trance is a gentle altered state, somewhere between being fully awake and asleep. When you are hypnotized, you are in a type of trance. You are usually in a light trance when you daydream. We talk about "zoning out" in front of the television, and this, too, is a form of trance. During a trance, the conscious mind doesn't quite leave—although sometimes it feels that way—but it's occupied elsewhere, and the subconscious has freer reign.

Trance techniques make energy work easier because they allow you to bypass the logical, skeptical, "Mr. Spock" conscious mind and get access to the subconscious more easily. As I discussed in chapter 3, energy follows thought, and imprinting images on the subconscious begins to make the images a reality. So if you can use a trance state to lower the barriers to your subconscious and "convince" it that your goal is already reality, you're more likely to have success with your magic or whatever goal you are trying to achieve through trance work.

So, short of having someone swing a pocket watch in front of your face and say, "You are getting sleepy," how do you achieve a trance state? Just as with grounding, there are as many ways to enter a trance as there are people who want to do it. First of all, however, you'll need to set the stage.

When you are just beginning with trance work, the environment you choose to work in is important. As with the work you did in chapter 3, you'll want to find a quiet place where you can practice without interruption. It's especially important with trance work that you also feel safe in whatever place you choose. You're not in danger when you go into a trance, but you are more vulnerable to ambient energies because the conscious mind—which would normally trigger you to tune out unwanted energy, sounds, or other distractions—is on a little vacation when you trance. Speaking of distractions, if you have pets, make sure that they are shut out of the room you are working in. Many animals love energy work, and they can be pests (lovable pests, but still . . .) when you're trying to do trance work or magic. Whenever my husband sees massage clients at our house and forgets to lock her out, my old lady cat lies next to the client and touches him or her with her paws. She seems to love the vibe they give off when they're in a trance state.

Pick a place to do trance work in that is not only safe, but comfortable. Pull the blinds or curtains, and work in dim light. You pull the curtains and dim the lights when you're going to sleep, which is like a deeper trance state, so this helps to trigger your mind that the conscious part of it is checking out for a while. Working by candlelight is good because it's dark enough to be trance inducing but light enough to remind most people not to nod off. If you use a candle, make sure, however, that it is in a very safe place in a stable candle holder in case you do fall asleep.

You may want to play some music in the background during your trance work. Some people find that this helps them slip into trance more easily, while others find it distracting. The good thing about music is that it can reduce noises from outside the room, such as sounds from traffic or other people in the house, to just one noise by drowning them out. Then in turn you can tune out the music (it's easier to ignore one noise than it is to ignore several) or listen to it, as you choose. This works especially well with headphones. If you want to try using music, choosing something repetitive is often helpful because after it has heard a few bars of the music, the brain becomes accustomed to it and won't be stimulated by the introduction of new sounds or melody changes. We have a tape of some Tibetan monks chanting "Om" that we use as background sound. It's terribly boring to listen to by itself, but the repetitive sound is great for inducing trance. It's also good to choose instrumental music so your conscious brain doesn't interrupt your trance by trying to follow the lyrics.

Once you've got the room set up, sit comfortably, ground, and raise your shield. With your conscious "security guard" mind sipping mojitos on the beach, it's best to turn on the alarm system, just in case. Again, you are not shielding because you need to worry about attracting negative energy, but because you want to keep out distracting energies and sounds. You can adjust your shield to filter out noise as well as energy. It's your shield, after all; it's as real as you make it, and you can "program" it to do whatever you need it to do.

Next, close your eyes or allow them to focus softly (let your eyes relax and your vision go blurry), and take several deep breaths. Feel your body relax with each breath. Then, when you are grounded and relaxed, try one of the following trance-inducing techniques. Before you start, however, if you're worried that you're going to "trance out" so far that you will have trouble coming back, there are two simple things you can do. Set an alarm clock to go off after a certain period of time (5–10 minutes for your first attempt; 15–20 if you're pretty good at trancing). You can also ask someone to knock on the door at a specific time. The noise of the clock or the knock should startle you out of the trance. It's not likely that you'll "go somewhere" and not be able to come back, but if you're afraid it might happen, your fear can interfere with your trance session.

Here is a short list of trance inducers. Bear in mind that this is another situation where the technique that works best for you will be the one that you make up, so use these ideas as a springboard to finding your own methods.

A Few Basic Ways to Induce Trance

DO SQUARE BREATHING. Breath exercises are great for energy and trance. To do square breathing, breathe in slowly for four counts, hold the breath for four counts, exhale for four counts, hold for four counts, and keep going. The counts should be very slow. The combination of breathing and counting will help you enter a light altered state.

LIGHT A CANDLE. Allow your eyes to soft-focus, then gaze at the flickering flame. You can do the same if you're sitting around a campfire or in front of a fireplace, but make sure you're safe first. It never, ever hurts to have a fire extinguisher around when you are doing anything with candles or flame.

BOWL OF WATER. Gaze at the surface of water in a bowl or at the flame of a candle reflected in the water.

THE NOTEBOOK. Close your eyes and visualize a notebook with lined paper. In your mind, write on one line of the paper, "I am in a trance." Visualize forming each letter of the sentence. Keep writing the sentence on subsequent lines.

THE MAZE. Close your eyes and imagine that you are in a maze of winding corridors. Like Theseus in the story about the minotaur, you've got one end of a golden string in your hand. The string winds through the passages to the center. Follow the string to the center. When you get there, you will be fully in trance.

THE STAIRCASE. Imagine climbing up or down a spiral staircase, each loop bringing you deeper into trance.

BURN MUGWORT INCENSE. This works in two ways. First, mugwort has some compound in it that seems to induce trance. It's not like smoking marijuana or taking a drug. It's subtle (and legal). It's good for magical work because it will help you trance, but you'll still have control. You can also use soft focus with the smoke to induce trance.

THE CRYSTAL. Find a chunk of crystal with many points or a rock with lots of random markings. Soft-focus, and gaze at the points or markings. You can also gaze at the reflection of candlelight off the facets.

TRICKLING WATER. If you have a tabletop fountain, soft-focus, then watch the bubbling water. Note that the sound of running water makes some people suddenly have to go to the bathroom, which isn't terribly helpful when you're trying to trance.

SWIRLING WATER. Visualize water swirling down a drain, or go run some water and watch the real thing. See the bathroom caveat from the trickling-water idea.

WATCH THE FISH. Allow your eyes to soft-focus, and gaze at an aquarium of fish. Yes, this sounds funny, but it really works! There is a reason that many Asians keep fish tanks in their homes—fish tanks have great energy (chi) and they're very relaxing. The day my husband and I moved, we and the group of friends who helped us were so tired that we sat in the living room and zoned out in front of the fish tank for several minutes before any of us realized that we'd fallen into some sort of fish-and-fatigue-induced hypnotic thrall.

THE SPIRAL. Draw a spiral on a piece of paper, and trace the spiral with your finger. Watch the tip of your finger as it goes around and around. This is best done in candlelight. I have a flat clay spiral with fingertip-sized grooves in it just for this purpose. Note that some people who are first beginning have trouble trancing and doing something physical—like moving their fingers—at the same time, so it might be best to start with one of the other ideas.

A Few More Advanced Ways to Induce Trance

These are "more advanced" because they require movement, training, or both.

DRUMMING. Beating a drum slowly induces trance because it is repetitive and it generates a wonderful, relaxing vibration. Don't drum quickly, because that raises energy instead of inducing trance. The idea is to imagine that your heart rate is slowing down with the speed of the drumming.

TRANCE DANCE. If you've ever been to a pagan or Wiccan event, you've probably seen people drumming and dancing around a fire. Dancing is one of the most fun ways to enter an altered state. You can do it alone, in the middle of a crowded club, or with your friends under the moonlight. Spinning—kind of like the Sufi "whirling dervishes" do—will put you in trance pretty quickly too, but be careful, please. It's easy to lose your balance and whack into the furniture (if you do this inside) or the fire (if you do it outside). If you're interested in trance dance, check out Gabrielle Roth's book *Sweat Your Prayers*.

TAI CHI AND CHI GUNG. If you have studied tai chi and/or chi gung, you know that these practices are meant to induce a light trance, among other things. My husband and I believe that they are so beneficial to learning about body, energy, and trance work that we require all of our students to learn a little of one or the other.

Turning Off the "Mind Chatter"

Concentration is central to good visualization, trance work, and magic. As I'm sure you discovered when you tried some of the trance exercises, sometimes it's hard to concentrate because your conscious mind is chattering away in the background—making a grocery list, reliving an argument with your ex, wondering what to pack for a trip—nattering on about whatever distracting thing it can obsess itself with at the time. Several of the trance-inducing techniques I just listed can help quiet the chattering mind, especially square breathing, listening to music with headphones, and the notebook, because they engage the brain enough that you can forget about the outside world, but not so much that you can't relax and trance. Here are a few additional things you can do before trance work or meditation to help turn off the chattering mind. There are many, many techniques for this, so if one of these doesn't work, try something new. You'll find the right one for you.

WRITE THE CHATTER OUT OF YOUR SYSTEM. Get a notebook and write down all of the gibberish going through your head. Write and write and write until it's purged. You can also imagine and visualize that you're writing it rather than actually writing.

WASH IT AWAY. Visualize yourself in a river current, with the water washing away all the extraneous stuff that is running through your head.

A VARIATION ON SQUARE BREATHING. Instead of slowly inhaling, holding, exhaling, and holding, do one full circuit slowly followed by a quick one, then alternate between the two.

THIRD EYE BREATHING. Breathe slowly and deeply, imagining that you're breathing from your third eye, the energy center in your forehead between your brows.

If you absolutely can't get the chatter to stop, it might mean that this isn't a good time for trance work because you have something important that you need to deal with. In this case, it may be best to deal with the outside issue first.

Trance with a Travel Guidebook: Meditation and Pathworking

Meditation and pathworking are extensions of the visualization and trance work you have already done. There are many types of meditation, but for our purposes, meditation is concentrating on an image or desired outcome while in a trance state. Pathworking is taking a mental journey while in a trance state.

Meditation

A meditation is somewhat like a prolonged visualization done under special circumstances. It's useful in magic and self-improvement because, as I explained earlier, when you concentrate on an image while in trance, it's easier to impress the image on your mind. Wiccans meditate on images for many reasons, including but not limited to the following:

TO EXERCISE THE MIND. Because it requires holding an image in the mind for a period of time, meditation can strengthen the ability to focus and sharpen awareness.

TO DO MAGIC OR HEAL. Both of these require concentration and visualization, which are both in turn aided by meditation and trance. Often, a Wiccan will meditate on the visualization of a goal—such as getting a new job—as part of a magical ritual to achieve that end. In addition to treating a sprained ankle medically, Wiccans may meditate on a mental image of the swelling going down. It's common for Wiccans to light a candle and meditate to help heal a loved one who is in the hospital.

TO "SET" A DREAM. This is sort of like a "call and response." You use a meditation to ask your subconscious a question right before bed. Then, when you go to sleep, the subconscious answers you in a dream.

TO GET PSYCHIC INFORMATION. This is similar to setting a dream, except the answer comes from other sources, such as a flash of inspiration or the psychic senses.

An Example of Using Meditation to Achieve a Goal

The following is an example of one process a Wiccan might use to achieve a goal with meditation. This is a framework that you can alter to use in a variety of circumstances.

Let's say you wanted to use meditation to improve your scores on the SAT or some other big test. You might follow these steps:

1. First, study for the test! Meditation is a powerful tool, but you must also work toward your goal on the mundane plane.
2. Choose a safe, quiet place to meditate. Turn off the phone. Put a "Do not disturb" sign on the door. Relax.
3. Create an image in your mind of you getting a great score on the test. This might be a mental picture of

someone shaking your hand and saying congratulations or a visual of the test-score number itself. The image that has the most meaning for you will be the one that works best.

4. Use one of the techniques from chapter 3 to ground. The taproot visualization is a great pre-meditation grounding technique.

5. Use one of the trance techniques from this chapter to enter a slightly altered state. The candle flame or bowl of water techniques might be particularly useful for this example.

6. Shift your consciousness from whatever technique you were using to enter the trance to the test-score image you chose. For example, if you're staring at a candle flame, "see" your image in the flame, visualize the flame becoming your image, or slowly allow your eyes to close and visualize your image in your mind's eye. Focus on the image. See the image become clearer. Make it real in your mind.

7. After a time, release the image and ground.

8. Repeat this once a day for several days to strengthen the image in your mind.

9. You can modify this process to work on any of the goals listed previously, and more.

Pathworking

Now that you have a bit of experience with concentrating on a single image, you can expand that experience into a pathworking. Just as in meditation, a pathworking begins by grounding, relaxing, and entering a trance state. However, once you've achieved trance, instead of focusing on a single image, you allow your mind to take you on a guided journey along a path or to a destination that you chose before you began. In chapter 1, I mentioned Mircea Eliade's work on shamanism and how the shaman uses altered states to travel on the world tree to the underworld or otherworld to get psychic or divine information. This is a form of pathworking. Wiccans use pathworking in the following ways, among others:

TO TALK TO THE GODS. The gods exist on earth, but it's easier to reach them on their own turf—the otherworld, the spirit realm. In meditation, you can travel to the worlds of the gods and learn about them in context. They may show or teach you things in a pathworking that would be difficult to experience on the mundane plane.

TO BUILD AN ASTRAL TEMPLE. An "astral temple," at least for the purposes of this book, is a place you create in your mind where you go to do magic or communicate with the gods, among other things. Pathworking to an astral temple usually involves taking multiple trips to this place, making it more concrete and clear each time you visit, until you can go there at will.

TO GET PSYCHIC INFORMATION. You can use a pathworking to meet helpful guides whom you can ask for information. For example, you might design a trip where you meet your inner self (a personification of the subconscious), and ask it to locate the source of pain in your body. Or you might visit the animal or human spirits of a sacred site to learn about the significance of the area. Likewise, you can use pathworking to meet, talk, and get information from the dead.

One of the most important things to remember when doing pathworking is that you must have a single starting place for your journeying, and that you must leave your pathworking the same way you came in. For example, some people visualize beginning their journey by going through a door or gate, and they pass back through the door or gate on their return to the "real," or mundane, world. Others imagine beginning at the mouth of a tunnel, and returning back through the tunnel at the end.

Retracing your steps is important because it signals your mind that you intend to come back to the mundane world. You want to make this clear to yourself so that you come back completely, and not with one foot in the otherworld and one foot on earth. When you are on a pathworking journey, your psychic or spirit self, not your physical self, is the one that makes the trip. You want to make sure that the psychic self reunites with the physical at the end of the pathworking. If they don't reconnect, you can feel disoriented, dizzy, queasy, muddled, or incomplete, for lack of a better word. Eliade posits that shamans are considered a little bit crazy because they are simultaneously in both worlds and therefore never completely in either. Do not panic, though —if you do pathworking and wander off track, you're not going to become a crazy shaman. If you have not managed to come completely back from a pathworking journey, you can fix the situation by returning into your pathworking through your gate or whatever visual you used, visualizing yourself reintegrating whatever part of you was left behind, and clearly and deliberately returning back the way you came, followed by a thorough grounding once you're back.

If you are truly worried about not being able to return, try the Theseus trick I discussed earlier in this chapter. When you enter the pathworking, tie a golden rope or thread to your gate or doorway and the other end to your wrist. If you get lost or disoriented in the pathworking, you can follow the thread home. (I've found the thread to be more reliable than a *Hansel and Gretel* trail of breadcrumbs.) Another option is to have someone stay in the room with you while you are pathworking. He or she can "talk you back" by verbally leading you to your entrance point if you get lost.

It's also important to use the same entry and exit point because you will ensure that your mind knows the place well and you can get there easily, especially if you didn't bring your golden thread. This makes it much simpler to get into your pathworking and find your way back. It also means that you can spend less time and energy with your "induction" (the beginning part of your trip that you repeat each time you journey) and more on the actual journey.

Setting Up a Pathworking

To set up a pathworking, first you must decide some of the particulars of your trip, such as the reason you are journeying, your path or destination, and whom or what, if anything, you'd like to encounter. Bear in mind that you may encounter all sorts of things you didn't plan for while journeying. You should also decide what image you'd like to use for your induction, or transition between the material world and your journey. You can use the door, gate, or tunnel ideas, or create your own.

When you've chosen these factors for your trip, you have the framework of a story. (There is a sample framework after this section.) The framework has three parts: the induction, which is the part where you enter the trance and pathworking; the "body," where you do whatever it is that you need to do in the pathworking; and the "closure," where you exit the pathworking. In many pathworkings, including the following sample, the induction and closure are closely scripted, but the body is not. This is because you can't plan for everything that happens in a pathworking. If you could, there would be no point in going.

Write down your framework. Once you have done this, you may want to read it into a tape recorder so you can use the sound of your own voice to guide you into your pathworking. Be sure to read very slowly and clearly, and pause for a bit after the induction and before the actual journey starts. If you don't want to tape yourself, you can ask a friend to record your induction instead, or when you get to the actual journey, you can have him or her read the induction to you, or you can simply imagine the starting point for yourself.

The steps for a pathworking are very similar to those of a meditation:

1. Choose a safe, quiet place to do your work. Turn off the phone. Put a "Do not disturb" sign on the door. Relax.
2. Use one of the grounding techniques from chapter 3 to ground, preferably one that requires no props.
3. Close your eyes, if they're not closed already. Turn on your tape recorder, tell your friend to start reading, or begin to visualize the entry point into your journey. Listening to or imagining the induction of your story should serve as a trance-inducer in most cases. However, if you find you are having trouble shifting consciousness, try square breathing while you are listening.
4. Listen to the induction. See yourself at your door or gate or tunnel. Take a moment to fix that place in

your mind. See yourself reaching out to touch the door, gate, or tunnel. Feel how real it is.

5. Once the image of your starting point is solid in your mind and you have achieved a light trance state, begin your journey.

6. As you experience your pathworking, pay careful attention to the details that you see, touch, smell, hear, and taste, and tell yourself that you will remember them even after you have finished the pathworking and are no longer in a trance state. Sometimes the information we receive in pathworkings is subtle and contained in the small things we encounter rather than in the large ones.

7. If you encounter anyone in your pathworking—humans, gods, fairies, elves, animal spirits, ghosts, folklore characters, or any other being—be polite! Don't touch or pet anything that doesn't want to be touched or petted, and if someone or something tells you to leave something alone, do so. The beings you find in a pathworking operate on a different plane, and the etiquette is different there. If you are respectful and take the time to examine a situation for clues as to how you should behave, the beings you encounter are more likely to help you and be receptive to your returning. Think of it as attending a formal dinner in a foreign country where you don't know the language

or customs, and approach it accordingly. And never, never, take anything unless it is obvious that it has been given to you. If you were at that formal dinner, after all, you wouldn't steal the forks. Items pilfered from spiritual realms, and/or the owners of those items, tend to come back to haunt the thief later, so it's a matter of common sense as well as etiquette.

8. When your journey is complete, return to your starting point. Shift your consciousness to the "real" world, and ground. As with meditation and trance, if you think you may have trouble coming back, ask a friend to rouse you gently from your trance at the end, or set an alarm clock to go off at a certain time. Neither of these techniques takes the place of grounding, though. Always ground after pathworking.

The following is the sample pathworking framework. For this sample, I am assuming that you will be either reading the script into a tape recorder or having someone read it to you. Note that pathworkings can be more structured than this one, with nearly every piece choreographed, or they can be much less structured, consisting of an induction, a period of time for you just to wander around and experience whatever there is to be experienced, and a return. As with everything in Wicca, you will want to experiment to see what level of detail you want to include in your pathworking script. I've put pauses in the script for the person reading the script. They are not meant to be read out loud. I have also noted where the induction, body, and closure begin and end so you have a frame of reference for creating your own.

Sample Pathworking

[Beginning of induction.] *Close your eyes and relax.* Pause. *Breathe deeply. Allow your body to relax more and more with each breath, until you are very relaxed, but not asleep.* Pause. *Allow yourself to slip gently into a trance state. If necessary, try square breathing until you are fully relaxed and in a trance.* Pause.

Focus on my voice and my words. Breathe. Relax. Pause. *You are going to take a journey in your imagination, your mind's eye. To begin, see or imagine that you are standing at the edge of a thick forest at night. You can hear the rustle of the wind in the leaves of the trees, and a full moon glows overhead. In the moonlight, you can clearly make out a path that begins right in front of you and leads off into the forest. To the right of the path, just at the beginning, is a tower of stones set one on top of the other. The tower is about three feet tall, and the stones that form it are roughly the size of cinder blocks. Sitting on top of the tower is a glowing lantern. This tower is your starting and ending point for this pathworking. Touch the tower and know that it is real.* Pause.

Begin walking down the path into the forest. Do not take the lantern with you, because you will not need it. The moon lights your path, so you have no difficulty finding your way. You can feel the soft earth beneath your feet. The trees are tall and dark, but this is not a frightening forest. It is somehow familiar, comforting. You walk on and on, toward the center of the forest. Pause.

Soon the path gives way to a large clearing, illuminated by the moonlight. You can see the blips of fireflies in the grass along the edge. In the center of the clearing, there is a large, flat stone—large enough for you to sit on. You walk into the clearing and sit on the stone, under the moonlight. You realize that you are in a sacred place. Pause. [Note: This is the end of the induction—the part of the pathworking that leads you into trance and into the sacred place where the work will be done.]

[Beginning of body.] *From your place on the flat rock, you see a woman emerging from the trees. As she walks across the clearing toward you, you notice that she is wearing a flowing white dress and a silver band with a crescent moon on her forehead. It is difficult to tell how old she is. As she walks slowly toward you, you are not afraid. In fact, you are filled with anticipation, knowing that this woman bears knowledge or information for you. The woman stops in front of you. Listen to what she has to tell you.* Long pause. [Leave enough time for the person doing the pathworking to hear the whole message.]

When the woman finishes speaking, you thank her. She turns and walks back across the clearing to disappear between the trees once more. [End of body.]

[Beginning of closure/exit from the pathworking.] *When you are ready, stand and begin walking across the clearing toward the path that you took to get here. When you find the trail in the bright moonlight, begin walking back to your starting point. As you walk, remember the details of the message that the woman gave you. You walk on and on, enjoying the warm night and the beautiful forest.* Pause. *Ahead, you see the glow of the lantern, and you know you are almost back. You approach the edge of the forest and the glowing lantern, and touch the tower of stones. When you touch the stones, you immediately and completely return to the mundane world.* [End of closure.]

Note that in this particular framework, whatever happens in the clearing is the work of the pathworking, and the parts where you walk the path to and from the clearing are meant to bring you in and out of trance. Try this pathworking a few times, and then begin modifying it or writing your own. Consider going to the clearing and meeting whoever or whatever is there, instead of the woman. Or do a spell using the flat stone in the clearing as an altar. The only limit on the possibilities is your imagination.

You may wish to journal about the experiences you have and the messages you receive. Over time, a pattern may emerge from the messages, or they may link up to form a larger message. In addition, just as with dreams, it can be hard to remember details of a pathworking after you've returned, and the bits that you do remember tend to disappear over time. (This happens in ritual too. We call it "circle memory"—which is really "circle forgetfulness.") If you write down the details immediately after your pathworking, you're more likely to retain the information.

Now that you know something about the basic mental tools that serve as a foundation for Wiccan practice, it's time to dig into the practice itself.

5

The Circle:

A Wiccan's Sacred Space

Wiccan rituals and magical workings are most often conducted in circles. The circle is sacred space, just like a church or temple, but created with energy and visualization. The circle symbolizes many things, but one of the most commonly held ideas is that it is a space "between" the material and spiritual worlds, since Wiccans walk, work, and worship in both. The circle is a place where both worlds exist and neither exists. It is a place outside of time and space.

Why Do You Need a Circle?

In addition to demarcating sacred space, the boundary of the circle works a little bit like your personal shield. When you draw the circle, you can decide what is allowed to enter it and what isn't. It can keep out everything, or it can be like a semi-permeable membrane that only allows certain things to pass. Some Wiccans draw circles around themselves before doing visualization or meditation because they believe that the circle will filter out extraneous sounds and energies that might interfere with their work. Others believe that the circle prevents negative entities or energies from entering the sacred space; in effect, the sacred space is safe space. This idea has at least one of its roots in ceremonial magic. When they are invoking spirits, ceremonial magicians may stand inside the circle for protection from whatever they're calling up. They may also stand outside the circle and cause the spirit to appear inside it, again for their own protection or to keep the spirit bound in one place. Most Wiccans don't work with the kind of spirits that you'd want to contain (and some Wiccans consider containing otherworldly beings rude), so this application isn't as relevant to us, but it's worth knowing.

Wiccans often raise energy in ritual in order to do magic, and the circle keeps that energy in place until it is released to achieve whatever purpose it was intended for. After all, you wouldn't want to go to all the trouble of raising energy only to have it seep out all over the place before you could use it. One thing the circle definitely retains is heat—from the bodies of the people standing in it, from any candles burned inside it, from energy, or from all of the above. If you were to reach out of the circle during a rite, you'd notice that the air outside the circle is cooler than it is inside. The edge of the circle itself has an energetic feel too. I don't recommend reaching out of the circle, however! Crossing the boundary of a circle before the circle is "taken down" is considered bad etiquette. It disregards the sacredness of the space, breaks concentration, and it may punch a hole in the circle that lets in (or out) things that the ritualgoers didn't intend.

It can have other wacky effects too. Once my coven was doing a guided visualization (a pathworking) in circle, and one of the members, stretching out on the floor to relax, accidentally put his feet outside the circle. In his pathworking, his feet were cold while the rest of his body was hot, and he couldn't move because they were "stuck" to the ground. He didn't figure out why he couldn't move until we ended the pathworking and he realized where his feet were. This had no long-term bad effects on him except that we teased him about it a lot.

Marking the Circle

A Wiccan circle can be marked on the floor indoors with chalk, paint, or a round rug. It can be etched into the ground and/or outlined with natural things like cornmeal or stones if it is outside. Some circles are very ornate, with magical symbols drawn around or inside them. Many circles, however, have no physical outline. They are simply drawn with energy. Some Wiccan traditions have customs about how large a circle should be, but many Wiccans just draw their circles large enough to hold everyone participating in the ritual or small enough to fit in the living room or wherever the ritual will be held.

When Do You Need a Circle?

You should draw a circle whenever you are going to do a Wiccan ritual that involves worship of the gods. Again, this is because the circle is sacred space. You do not have to use a circle in magical working, although, as I already mentioned, it will help you focus your concentration and energy and keep out distractions. You also do not have to use a circle during meditation or pathworking, but many people feel safer doing trance work with that magical boundary around them. The choice is yours.

Preparing the Space

It is fairly common practice amongst Wiccans to "cleanse" the area where they are going to hold their ritual both physically and psychically before drawing the circle. Cleansing the space has several benefits. First of all, it's more respectful to conduct religious or magical work in a physically clean space. It's less distracting to draw a circle and focus on a rite in a space that's psychically clean and devoid of whatever unwanted energy has accrued throughout the day from arguments, your mother-in-law's visit, and so on. Cleansing the space beforehand also helps focus your mind on the upcoming ritual. For some people, cleansing the space becomes a trigger that gets their brains into "ritual mode" before the circle is even cast.

Begin by cleaning the physical space. If your rite is going to be outside, clear anything that might be in the way, like branches, children's toys, or lawn tools; rake up stray leaves and twigs; and check for anything that you might trip over. If you like to do ritual barefoot, check for sticker plants too! If your ritual will be inside, move furniture if necessary and vacuum or sweep the floor. Vacuuming and sweeping not only clean the floor, but they help break up and disperse energy. Using special ritual cleaner made from clean water and specially selected herbs is a cool idea too. Mixing up the cleaner is a magical act in itself. Just don't put essential oils in it. They can take the finish off hardwood floors.

Next, cleanse the space psychically. There are many techniques for doing this, but here are some of the easier and more common ones. Choose the one that seems most appropriate for you and your space.

- Sweep out anything energetic that you don't want in the space with a special ritual broom. You do not have to touch the floor with the broom, so it can work in a room with carpet or even outside. As you sweep, visualize the broom pushing out any extraneous or unwanted energy. This technique is very common.
- Ring a special bell in each corner of the room, or in each direction if you're outside. The sound of a good bell is great for dispelling energy. Rattles also work well.
- "Smudge," or purify, the area with an incense burner full of smoldering dried herbs. In the United States, we most often associate smudging with the Native American custom of using the smoke of burning desert sage

to cleanse a space or a person's aura. However, many cultures use smoke or incense to clear ritual areas. Even the Catholic Church—referred to by some of my Catholic friends as the "bells and smells" church—uses ritual purification incense. You can use any herb of your choice, but make sure to *look up all herbs before burning them.* Some of them are toxic, and you don't want to breathe in their smoke. (See the recommended reading list in the back of this book for titles of herb books.) If you are preparing a large outdoor ritual space and you need a lot of smoke, try making a censer out of an old coffee can. It's not pretty, but it works! Punch several holes in the sides of the can with a screwdriver or more appropriate tool. (When we did this, we were in the middle of the Mexican desert, and a screwdriver was all we had.) Punch two holes opposite each other near the rim of the can, and thread a piece of wire or wire hanger through them to make a handle, like a child's sand bucket. Make sure the handle is long so whoever is holding the censer doesn't singe their hands because they're too close to the stuff you'll be burning in the can. Put a few hot coals in the bottom of the can, and add a handful of dried herbs. When the herbs are smoking, walk around your sacred space, swinging the can gently to spread the smoke. Add more herbs as necessary.

- Sprinkle the area with saltwater. Salt and water are used for purification in cultures across the world. Some Wiccan rituals call for saltwater to be sprinkled inside the circle during the ritual, but that doesn't mean you can't use it beforehand too.
- Sweep out the space with a paper fan. The movement of the fan breaks up stagnant energy.
- Use visualization to clear the space. Visualize the wind pushing out any unwanted psychic residue, even if you're inside. It's a visualization, after all, so the laws of nature don't have to apply. You can combine visualization with one of the other cleansing techniques too.

Casting the Circle

Casting the actual circle is a lot simpler than you might believe after all of these preparations. Before I get to the instructions, though, you should know a little bit about the athame—a Wiccan's ritual knife—and the wand. We'll cover these tools in more depth in chapter 8. You can draw a circle without any tools whatsoever, but many Wiccans use an athame or wand. The purpose of the tools in this case is to focus the energy you'll be raising to a point, like a pencil, from which you draw the circle. However, I think it's very important to learn how to cast a circle without tools before learning with tools. If you can do it without tools, you can do it anywhere, and that's handy in an emergency or when you need to do spell or trance work on the fly. Doing it without tools also reinforces the fact that the tools are just focal points, and the real power comes from the energy you draw and your own mind.

To cast a circle:

1. Choose a place along what will be the edge of your circle to begin. Many Wiccans choose to begin in one of the cardinal directions: east, south, west, or north. We'll talk about the directions and why you might choose one over another in more detail in the next chapter, but for learning purposes, you can choose any quarter you wish. Most Wiccans begin in the east, because it's where the sun rises, or the north, because it's associated with the earth, and the circle is drawn with earth power. There is no reason, however, why you can't start anywhere along the edge of your space that you want.
2. Ground.
3. Visualize your taproot, and then visualize drawing energy up from the earth's core through the taproot.
4. Extend the index and middle fingers of whichever hand you prefer, and visualize the energy flowing into those fingers. Although some Wiccans think you should use your dominant hand for this (assuming you have a dominant hand), either hand works just fine.

5. Begin to move clockwise around your space and visualize the energy flowing through you and forming the circle. Many people find it helpful to visualize the stream of energy in a particular color. Wiccans almost always move clockwise, or sunwise, in a circle because it mimics the path of the sun. Some Wiccans believe that moving counterclockwise, or "widdershins," "undoes" the circle. Move slowly, and concentrate. Remember to breathe deeply. Don't hold your breath!

6. When you have gone all the way around the circle and returned to your starting point, stop walking and solidify the circle by visualizing the entire boundary in your mind. When you can "see" it in your mind's eye, extend the circle above your head and below the ground or floor so it is a three-dimensional bubble around you rather than a two-dimensional circle on the floor. Hold the image in your mind for a few moments to strengthen it and make it real. Remember, energy follows thought, so the visualization is very important.

You've just cast a simple circle. Once you have practiced this and have the hang of it, you can try casting the circle without moving or using your fingers. You can also practice drawing it with a wand or athame.

Once you're inside the circle, do not cross the boundary. You do not want to break up the energy. If you need to leave the circle and come back in, use the two fingers you used to draw the circle to cut a "door" in the boundary. When you return, redraw the line. Try not to do this except in an emergency, though. It's hard to maintain the energy of the circle if you leave it, and it messes up your focus on whatever work you're doing in the circle. Some Wiccans consider it unwise to allow a circle to stand empty, in which case someone new must come into the circle if the lone occupant goes out.

To take down the circle at the end of your ritual, begin at your starting point and move around the edge counterclockwise as you visualize drawing up the circle through your two fingers and pushing it back into the earth through your taproot. *Do not allow the energy to stay in your body.* Return it to the earth. Ground after taking down the circle.

In the next chapter, we'll explore the four quarters and the four elements, which Wiccans use to strengthen their circles and their magic.

6

The Four Elements and the Four Quarters

In Wiccan and magical thought, the energy that is infused throughout the universe can be divided into four elements: earth, air, fire, and water. The elements are the building blocks of life; the forces of nature and creation. If one were missing, the world as we know it would not exist.

Wiccans work with the elements in many ways. They incorporate elemental energy into their circles, rituals, and spells. They attune themselves to the elements in order to work in concert with the rhythms of nature. They also study the elements to learn more about themselves and the world around them. Some of the secrets of the universe are locked in the elements.

Each element has its own "feel"; its own energetic signature. Each also has several associations, or correspondences. These correspondences are useful in magic. The idea behind working with correspondences is the "like attracts like" concept we covered earlier. Fire attracts things associated with fire. Water attracts things associated with water, and so on. Therefore, if your goal and one of the elemental energies share traits in common, incorporating that element into your spell work or ritual would strengthen your effort. It may seem surprising how many things are associated with each element, but if you think back to the idea that the elements are the building blocks of life, then it's not such a stretch.

Here is a brief list of elemental correspondences. This is by no means complete, since everything under the sun (and the sun itself) has an elemental correspondence. However, it will do to get you started working with the elements and give you a taste of each.

THE ELEMENT OF EARTH is feminine, solid, and stable. It corresponds to the north; winter and the Winter Solstice; the astrological signs Taurus, Virgo, and Capricorn; midnight; the dark of the moon/waning moon; old age and/or death; fertility; money; stability; building foundations; food and sustenance; and agriculture and gardening. Some of the colors associated with it are green, black, gray, and brown, and some of the animals associated with it are the bear and buffalo. Wiccans often use rocks, crystals, or salt to represent earth in their rituals.

THE ELEMENT OF AIR is masculine, light, and cerebral. It corresponds to the east; spring and the Spring Equinox; the astrological signs Gemini, Libra, and Aquarius; the dawn; the new moon; birth; youth; enlightenment; inspiration; communication; writing; mobility; and computers and electronics. Some of the colors associated with it are yellow and gold, and some of the animals associated with it are insects and birds, especially eagles and hawks. Wiccans often use incense smoke or feathers to represent air in their rituals.

THE ELEMENT OF FIRE is masculine, hot (obviously), and energetic. It corresponds to the south; summer and the Summer Solstice; the astrological signs Aries, Leo, and Sagittarius; noon or midday; the waxing moon; adolescence; impetuousness; passion; drive; creativity; anger; force; light and brightness; and transformation. Some of the colors associated with it are red and orange, and some of the animals associated with it are horses and lions. In their rituals, Wiccans use fire to symbolize itself.

THE ELEMENT OF WATER is feminine, cleansing, and healing. It corresponds to the west; fall and the Fall Equinox; the astrological signs Cancer, Scorpio, and Pisces; dusk; the full moon; adulthood; nurture; emotions; the subconscious; the otherworld; transformation (like fire, but slower); mystery; compassion; secrets; and the occult. Some of the colors associated with it are blue and green, and some of the animals associated with it are fish and dolphins. In their rituals, Wiccans use water to symbolize itself.

Beings of the Elements

Many Wiccans believe that there are spirits or other otherworldly beings that are associated with each element. How Wiccans perceive what those spirits are, what they look like, and their powers or properties varies depending on the Wiccan and/or his or her tradition.

In the old magical grimoires, which are really the providence of ceremonial magicians and not Wiccans, the beings of the earth are called gnomes, the air beings are called sylphs, the fire beings are called salamanders, and the water beings are called undines. The gnomes, unsurprisingly, have a grounded, solid energy, and are thought to be stewards of the earth and keepers of its treasures, like precious metals and minerals. The sylphs are light and elusive and are believed to ride on the wind and inspire new thought and fresh ideas. The salamanders live in the coals of the campfire, and enhance passion and the creative "spark." The undines are lithe and full of grace and mystery, flowing with the water in which they live.

Some Wiccans use the ceremonial magic system and refer to the beings of the elements by those names. Personally, I don't see the elemental beings as gnomes, sylphs, salamanders, and undines, although they certainly share traits with them. For me, the beings associated with the elements are more nebulous, and their forms and strengths more flexible, but they are not less powerful. In my perception, they don't have the solidity (if you can call a sylph solid) that the ancient names imply. We do not teach the gnome/sylph/salamander/undine idea to our students, but they are certainly welcome to use that system if it works for them. As I said, each Wiccan experiences the elementals in his or her own way. If you decide to walk the Wiccan path, you will discover your own relationship with the elementals.

I should also point out here that many Wiccans associate certain gods and goddesses with each element. The Celtic goddess Brid, for example, might be a fire goddess because she is goddess of the forge. There is more about the gods in chapter 7, and after you read that, you might want to explore this idea for yourself.

Attuning with the Elements

Many Wiccans put a good deal of time and effort into exploring and aligning themselves with the elements in order to enhance their rituals and magic. The following are a few easy exercises that you can do to begin attuning yourself to the elements. They're so easy, in fact, that they're kind of obvious. That's the point, for two reasons. First, the elements are everywhere and in everything, so getting in sync with them *should* be simple. The second reason is that because they're everywhere and in everything, we take them for granted. Sometimes shifting our perception slightly and making a conscious decision to become more aware of something ubiquitous, like the elements, opens up whole new possibilities right under our noses, in our everyday lives. Try one or more of these ideas:

EXPERIENCE THE ELEMENTS AT HOME. Find and list everything in your living space that symbolizes one of the elements to you. For example, the stove, the microwave, the fireplace, the space heater, the curling iron, the hair dryer, the toaster oven, matches, a cigarette lighter, the thermostat, the furnace, the barbeque, the electric blanket, and maybe even the smoke detector all represent fire. Once you've made your list, reflect on why you chose the things you did. What do they have in common? How are they different? Repeat for the other three elements.

EXPERIENCE THE ELEMENTS OUTDOORS. Visit a natural place that contains or symbolizes to you one of the elements. For example, you could go to a garden, forest, or cave for earth; a windy bluff for air; or a stream, lake, or ocean for water. If you can't find a suitably fiery place (I live near a volcano; you may not be so fortunate), a campfire somewhere away from city noise and people is a great alternative. Relax and ground in the place you chose. Close your eyes, unless it's not safe. Breathe in deeply. Use as many of your senses as possible to experience the element. See if you can touch it (not fire, of course, although you can pass your hand near it and feel the heat), smell it, hear it, taste it. Spend enough time in your chosen location to make a real connection to the element. Write down your perceptions afterward. Repeat with the other three elements.

EXPERIENCE THE ELEMENTS IN YOUR MIND. Create a pathworking where you visit each element and learn about it. For example, journey to the bottom of the sea or the surface of the sun. Record your experience, and repeat for the other three elements. Instructions for creating a pathworking are in chapter 4.

EXPERIENCE THE ELEMENTS THROUGH THE SEASONS. You may have noticed in the correspondence list that each element is associated with a season. To Wiccans, the cycle of the seasons throughout the year is one of the most important things that the elements symbolize. As you'll see in chapter 9, the Wiccan holidays are based on the seasonal cycles. To attune yourself to the elements and seasons together, choose one of the solstices or equinoxes to begin. From that day until the next solstice or equinox, make a conscious effort to notice and feel how the associated element works in your life and how it aligns with its season. For example, begin to explore spring and air, separately and together, beginning on the Spring Equinox, and keep it up until the Summer Solstice, when you will shift your attention to summer and fire. Follow the cycle through the year. Record what you discover.

The Quarters

In addition to being associated with a season, each element is associated with a cardinal direction. Earth is north, air is east, fire is south, and water is west. The four directions, also called the four quarters, are an integral part of Wiccan ritual and magic.

If you picture a magic circle, like the one you learned to draw in chapter 5, and place the four quarters in their proper places around it, the circle becomes a microcosm of the universe. All of the elements of life are present. If you start in the east quarter and move clockwise around the circle, you travel from dawn to midday to dusk to midnight, the cycle of a day; from new moon to waxing moon to full moon to waning moon, the cycle of the moon—a month; from spring to summer to fall to winter, the cycle of the sun—a year; and from birth to adolescence to adulthood to old age, the cycle of a human life.

Since Wiccans strive to work with natural patterns, they "call" the quarters into their ritual circles. By doing this, they bring the cycle of the seasons and all of the building blocks of life into their microcosm. If you subscribe to the idea of the circle as a space "between the worlds," then you are bringing together the material and spiritual worlds and manifesting your will on the spiritual plane. Bringing the quarters into the circle packs a wallop for your ritual or magic, and many Wiccans wouldn't build a circle without them.

Calling the Quarters

Wiccans often call the quarters in ritual just after the circle is drawn. Frequently, they will draw the circle and then go around it twice more, sprinkling saltwater one time and carrying burning incense the other. This brings the four elements into the circle, since saltwater represents earth and water and burning incense represents fire and air. If the elements are already there before the quarters are called, it's easier to call the quarters because like attracts like. To clarify: The elements and the quarters are not the same thing. However, they are tied tightly together by symbolism. As to whether the elements represent the quarters, the quarters represent the elements, or both, you'll have to decide for yourself. There are Wiccans in all three camps.

Before we plunge into quarter calling, you should know a little bit about the witches' symbol: the pentagram. A pentagram is a five-pointed star. Four of the points represent the elements, and the fifth represents spirit or deity, which unites them all. If the pentagram is in a circle, as you see in a lot of Wiccan jewelry, it represents the four elements and spirit bound by the magic circle. I've also heard it said that the pentagram is the human hand and the points are the fingers, so in this case it represents human potential. The pentagram has been linked to Satanism and all sorts of other unsavory things by Hollywood scriptwriters and others who have no clue what they're talking about, but it is really a powerful and positive symbol of creation and vitality.

When you call the quarters using the following method, you will draw an invoking pentagram in the air in front of you in each quarter, using your fingers or an athame as you did to draw a circle in chapter 5. An invoking pentagram is used to summon or invite the energy of the quarter to the circle. Just as you did with the circle, you will visualize yourself pulling energy from the earth and inscribing the pentagram with the energy and your fingers or athame. Although a pentagram is a pentagram, it is drawn differently in each quarter. For example, to draw an invoking pentagram for earth, you begin at the top point and draw down and to the left, then up and to the right. For fire, you begin at the top point and draw down and to the right, then up and to the left, and so on.

Just to make things confusing, there is also one "banishing" pentagram for each quarter that you draw when you take down the circle. Banishing pentagrams are meant to "release" or "dismiss" the quarter energy. Personally, I don't like the word banishing because it's rude. After all, the quarters and elementals are helping you, and you're not kicking them out of your circle or sending them to bed without supper when you're through. But banishing is the commonly accepted term, so you should know it. You could call these the "hello" and "goodbye" pentagrams, but that sounds far cheesier and less mysterious. The following diagram illustrates how to draw the pentagrams.

Invoking Pentagrams

Banishing Pentagrams

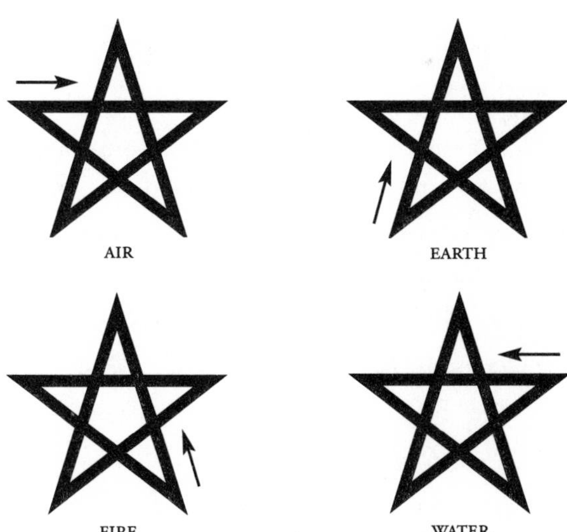

Arrows show the point on which to start and the direction in which to draw.

One more thing before we get into the actual method: If you just can't remember eight different pentagram-drawing methods, there is a way to "cheat." Use the earth-invoking pentagram at each quarter when calling, and the earth-banishing pentagram at each when you're taking down the circle. Several groups that I have worked with have done this, and it works just fine. The point is not whether or not you can remember eight different pentagrams. It is your will, visualization, and intent that are important.

There are many ways to call the quarters into a circle. Here is one easy method:

1. Cleanse your ritual space, ground, and draw your circle as you learned in chapter 5.

2. Stand in your circle, facing outward, in one of the quarters. Most Wiccans start either in the north or in the east, for reasons that I explained in chapter 5. For the sake of this example, I'm going to pretend you're starting in the east.

3. Draw your air-invoking pentagram with your fingers or athame. Visualize the energy flowing from the earth, through your body, down your arm, and out your fingers or athame. Visualize the pentagram forming in the air as you draw it. You may wish to see the energy as a specific color. Many Wiccans use yellow for east, red for south, blue for west, and green for north. In my group, we use white for all four. Use whatever color(s) makes sense for you.

4. Although you are "calling" the quarter with your energy, you can call verbally too. This is not essential or required, and sometimes the best quarter calls are completely silent. Most Wiccans do say something out loud, however. You can say it as you are drawing the pentagram, or, if that's too hard to do at the same time as the visualization, say it directly afterward. It can be as simple as "Welcome, powers of the east," "Powers of air, join us this night," or "I summon/call thee/you, powers of the east, to join/guard/protect our circle." The quarter call can be, and frequently is, a short poem that contains imagery the Wiccan associates with the quarter he or she is calling. Sometimes rhyme is helpful because it has a pattern, and the cadence induces a light trance as the words evoke images in the speaker's mind. However, I've heard a lot of poetry abuse done in the name of quarter calling, so if you think you can't write something eloquent that won't make you crack up in the middle of your call, stick with the simple stuff. There are examples of quarter calls in many Wiccan books, including works by Scott Cunningham and Starhawk, but I encourage you to write your own. They will mean more to you, and you will be able to imbue them with more energy.

5. When you are done drawing and speaking, spend a few moments visualizing the pentagram glowing brightly in front of you. If you can do it at the same time, try

visualizing or feeling something you associate with the quarter/element at the same time, such as seeing an eagle or feeling the wind blowing on your face. It's not easy to hold two visualizations at once, but if you take the time to figure it out, it will greatly enhance the energy of your call.

6. Continue to the south. Draw the south/fire-invoking pentagram and speak your invocation. Visualize it; make it real. Continue with the west/water and the north/earth.

When you have finished your ritual or magic, and before you take up the circle itself, you should "banish," release, or say farewell to the quarters. To do this:

1. Begin in the quarter where you started.
2. Draw the banishing pentagram for the appropriate element, visualizing the energy dispersing.
3. Say something like "Powers of the east, thank you for attending, and farewell," or make up your own statement. Try to say your farewell while you are drawing the banishing pentagram, but as with the call, if you can't do that, say it immediately afterward.
4. Visualize the last of the pentagram disappearing.
5. Move on to the next quarter, and repeat. Here you have two choices. You can go clockwise, as you did during the calling, or you can move counterclockwise. As I mentioned previously, some Wiccans feel

that moving counterclockwise in the circle "erases" the circle, but since you're taking it down anyway, it may be appropriate here. Actually, some Wiccans insist on moving counterclockwise when they banish the quarters. Again, experiment with both ways, and do whichever feels right to you.

The Witches' Pyramid

The Witches' Pyramid is a magical principle or philosophy that is closely tied to the quarters. The Pyramid contains four statements that express what you need to do to work effective magic and be a true Wiccan or witch. Each statement is associated with a quarter, and each quarter is represented as a tier or level of the Pyramid. Many witches study and work through each of the four statements in an effort to master their craft. They progress from the bottom tier (east), which is considered by many to be the easiest, upward through the south, west, and finally to north, which is often the most difficult. I present a short discussion of the levels of the Witches' Pyramid here because you are exploring the quarters. More information can be found in some of the books in the recommended reading list.

EAST—TO KNOW: This is the base of the Pyramid. Air is linked to knowledge. To work magic, Wiccans must know their will, intent, resources, and heart. They must also know that their magic or ritual will work. Here is where you ask yourself if Wicca is right for you.

SOUTH—TO DARE: This is the "scary" level of the Pyramid. Fire is linked to courage. To work magic and be a Wiccan, you have to dare. You have to dare to change, dare to be successful, dare to be different, dare to be strong. Here is where you ask yourself if you have the courage to walk your chosen path.

WEST—TO WILL: To work magic and be a Wiccan, you must know your will. Water is linked to inner knowing and the subconscious. This level is about gathering your power and making sure that your goal is aligned with your will or life purpose. Here you ask yourself if you have the focus, strength, and conviction to continue, and if continuing serves your higher purpose.

NORTH—TO KEEP SILENT: Many people, Wiccans included, are gabby by nature, so this level of the Pyramid is often the hardest. Earth is linked to quiet and death. To keep silent means that you don't discuss with others your magical work or the inner spiritual work that you do. It's an old magical principle that talking about magic dissipates it. Certainly, to keep silent for a Wiccan is also about safety; you may want to scream about your religion from the rooftops, but until Wicca is fully accepted in our society, you risk losing your job, family, home, and much more. In Wicca, for both of these reasons, discretion is the better part of valor. Here is where you ask yourself if you can keep your magic to yourself, and if you can stand to walk a spiritual path that you may not be able to discuss with your family and friends for fear of repercussion.

Now that you have the basic tools such as grounding and shielding, and you know the bare bones of building a circle and calling the quarters, it's time to meet the gods.

7

Getting to Know the Wiccan Gods

IN WICCA, THE DIVINE, or deity, is greater than creation, and yet it is creation. It is immanent in all things, but it is also distant and beyond our grasp. It is too vast for us to comprehend in its entirety, but we can begin to experience it through our relationship with the gods, who are facets of the divine. As I mentioned briefly in chapter 2, the two main aspects of deity that Wiccans work with are simply called the Goddess and the God. They are the female and male "halves" of the divine. In Wiccan thought, the union of the Goddess and God creates the universe. The relationship between the Goddess and God is symbiotic. Like darkness and light, each half needs the other to express itself fully. The God represents, among other things, power unmanifest; the spark of life. The Goddess gives this power form.

So are the gods real, sentient, independent entities? Are they masks that humans put on deity to understand it better, as Joseph Campbell suggests? Are they archetypes—symbols for universal themes that tend to pop up in the same way across cultures? Are they thoughtforms that have taken on energy as people have revered them over the years? Are they simply facets of our own psyches? Many Wiccans would tell you that the gods are all of those things—which are by no means mutually exclusive—and more.

The idea of a female and male polarity, which is what the Goddess and God are, is a bit abstract, but the Wiccan gods themselves—the faces Wicca puts on the two sides of the polarity—are not abstract at all to those who work with them. Wiccans have a deep love and respect for their gods, but they do not cower in front of them or beg favors. Wiccans work with their gods in a reciprocal partnership. Since in Wicca everyone is his or her own best priestess and no one comes between you and the gods, Wiccans have the responsibility and honor of forging bonds with the gods for themselves. A Wiccan's relationship to the gods can be very intimate and familiar. This doesn't mean that Wiccans will invite Thor and Freya to down a few brews while they watch the Super Bowl and eat Doritos, but it does mean that they talk directly to, work with, and get to know their gods at a level that is not nearly as easy to achieve in the framework of a large, mainstream religion.

So who are the Wiccan gods?

The Goddess

The Wiccan Goddess is the mother of all things. She is the earth, which births and sustains us and receives us again in death. She is the source of fertility and abundance. She is the great and nurturing mother, but, since all things must die, she also represents death, which is necessary for rebirth. The moon is the symbol of the Goddess. Like the moon, which has its waxing, full, waning, and new phases, the Goddess has many faces. She is energetic and full of potential like springtime, mature and fruitful like summer, aging and wise like autumn, and dark and silent like winter. Some Wiccans think of the Goddess as having three aspects—youthful maiden, fertile mother, and wise crone—and that she shows each of these faces in turn as the cycle of the year progresses. Others, like me, believe that she possesses and shows all of these attributes all of the time. She is the constant, eternal feminine principle. Some of her symbols are the moon, the cup or chalice, the cauldron, owls, cows, milk, silver, flowers, shells, and pearls.

The God

The God, sometimes called the Horned God, is the great hunter, the lord and steward of the animals and forests. He is often pictured with horns to show his affiliation with the earth's creatures. He is fierce and feral, wise and gentle. The sun is the God's symbol, and like the sun, without which the earth (and Goddess) would be barren, the God is the energetic principle. The God also represents sex and the urge to life. Many Wiccans link the God with the agricultural cycle: He is the spark of life that makes the seed sprout in the cold ground, the seedling that pushes its head from the earth, the ripened grain, and the harvest. He is also the lord of the underworld who tends souls from the time of death until they are ready for rebirth. Some of the symbols of the God are phalluses and phallic objects, such as spears, swords, arrows, and wands. Other God symbols are the color gold; horns or antlers and the stag, snakes, seeds and ripened grain, and the sickle.

The Goddess and God Together

The Goddess is the God's mother and lover. In the mythos of most Wiccans, the Goddess gives birth to the God, he matures, they make love and she becomes pregnant, he dies, and he is reborn of her again. The God's existence is cyclical, like the grains, animals, and humans he tends, and the Goddess's existence is constant, like the earth beneath our feet. The two are forever entwined throughout the mysteries of life, death, and rebirth.

Introducing Yourself to the God and Goddess

Communicating directly with the God and Goddess is one of the greatest joys and responsibilities of a Wiccan. You need not go to a church or sacred place to do this, as all places are sacred to them. The following is a simple ritual for introducing yourself to the Great Mother and the Horned

God. You can include both of them in one ritual, or, if you'd like, you can hold separate rituals for each one. Just modify the instructions accordingly. You will need an athame if you have one, a white or silver candle, a red or gold candle, holders for both candles, matches or a lighter, flowers, and acorns or pine cones.

1. Clean and clear your ritual space.

2. Ground.
3. Cast a circle. Do not call the quarters; the focus should be on the gods.
4. Sit in the center of the circle on the floor, with the candles in their holders in front of you. Light the white or silver candle, place the flowers next to it, and say something like:

   I light this for you, Great Goddess, Lady of the Moon, Mother of All Things. My name is ______, and I have come here to bring you this offering of flowers, know you better, and seek your wisdom.

   Note that you are not calling the Goddess into the circle. You'll do that later in the chapter. You are simply speaking to her.
5. Tell the Goddess something about yourself: why you are seeking her, what you might like to learn, why you are a Wiccan, etc.

6. When you have finished speaking, close your eyes and relax. Breathe deeply. Contemplate the Goddess and your relationship with her. Images may form in your mind's eye. Pay special attention to them, because they are your message from the Goddess. If nothing happens, or if you didn't "feel" the Goddess, don't worry! By lighting the candle and stating your intent, you have made yourself known to her. You may receive a message later in your dreams or visions, but the important thing is that you have made yourself known to her. You may need to do this ritual more than once to feel as though you have made contact at the level you would like to. That's okay. There are experienced Wiccans who do things like this to reconnect too, even though they may have been walking the path for decades. Be patient; remember that it's not only the Christian god who works in mysterious ways. Oftentimes with the Wiccan gods, things happen when they are meant to, and that's not necessarily on your predetermined schedule.

7. When the images are gone or you feel you are ready, open your eyes and say something like:

   Thank you, Great Goddess, for your gift of wisdom.

8. Light the gold or red candle, place the acorns or pine cones next to it, and say something like:

   I light this for you, Great God, Lord of the Sun, Lord of the Forest. My name is ________, and

I have come here to bring you this offering of acorns/pine cones, know you better, and seek your wisdom.

9. Note that as with the Goddess, you are not calling the God into the circle. You'll do that later in the chapter. You are simply speaking to him.

10. Tell the God something about yourself: why you are seeking him, what you might like to learn, why you are a Wiccan, etc.

11. Again, close your eyes and relax. Breathe deeply. Contemplate the God and your relationship with him. Images may form in your mind's eye. Pay special attention to them, because they are your message from the God. As with the Goddess, if nothing happens, don't worry! The important thing is that you have made yourself known to the God. You may receive a delayed-reaction message or small sign later as you go about your daily routine. Note that you may also have an easier time contacting the God than the Goddess, or vice versa. This can be for any number of reasons, including that you identify most with deity of one gender or the other or that the symbol set for one of them resonates with you more clearly.

12. When the images are gone or you feel like you are done, say something like:

Thank you, Great God, for your gift of wisdom.

13. Stand, take down your circle, and ground. If possible, take the lit candles, flowers, and acorns or pine cones and put them in a special place or on your altar (see chapter 8). If you can, allow the flames to burn for a while. Otherwise, snuff the candles. To deepen or expand on the experience, you can try the ritual again later with the same candles and add other elements.

The "Other" Gods

Think, for a moment, of a tree with a thick trunk that splits into two large branches. In turn, smaller branches grow from the large ones, and still smaller branches from the small ones, and so on. Deity is the trunk of the tree, and the God and Goddess are the two main branches. The smaller branches that fork off of the two big ones are the world's gods and goddesses; facets of the male or female half of deity. Note that there are some deities that are androgynous and don't fit easily into either gender category, but the majority are male or female, at least some of the time.

In addition to working with the God and Goddess, most Wiccans also work with one or more of these facets or faces of the masculine or feminine divine. For example, a Wiccan may ask the Greek goddess Aphrodite for help with a ritual designed to attract love or call the Egyptian goddess Bast to a ritual to find a lost cat. Both Aphrodite and Bast are faces of the Great Goddess, albeit very different faces, from different cultures and times.

If you are new to Wicca, you probably will want to work only with the Wiccan God and Goddess in ritual for a while. That way, you will get to know the specific Wiccan gods, get some practice with your ritual skills, and get an idea of what a Wiccan ritual "feels" like before you try to call a different god or goddess. Some Wiccans never call on other gods and just stick to the Great Goddess and God. Later in this chapter, there are some ideas for how to familiarize yourself with the gods and call them in a ritual circle.

Your Personal Deities

Many Wiccans have personal patron deities—in addition to the God and Goddess—that they work with frequently. They may call these patrons (or matrons) to every ritual they do or set up shrines to the patrons in their homes. Other Wiccans, as in my previous example, will call on gods or goddesses with particular attributes once in a while to help with certain rituals.

The choice of the gods that you work with in circle is very personal. No one else can tell you which ones you will resonate with and have the easiest time getting to know. The Celtic, Greek, Roman, Norse, and Egyptian gods are probably the most popular amongst Wiccans, but your deities may not belong to any of these cultures.

One of the best ways to find your gods or goddesses is to read mythology. Lots of mythology. There are some mythology book suggestions in the recommended reading list in the back of this book. As you read, which themes or stories stick with you? Which deities have traits that you'd like to attract into your life? Which deities, in their stories, dealt with a problem similar to one you are dealing with, or had experiences similar to yours? Which deities "call your name" as you read? Instead of picking one god, you may choose to work with a pantheon. A pantheon is the entire group of gods associated with a culture, for example, the Greek gods.

If you are drawn to a particular pantheon, one way to get to know those gods, and perhaps find the one that resonates with you best, is to visit the sacred sites of that pantheon. This is not always possible because of money or logistical constraints, but if you have the resources to do it, I highly recommend it. It is much easier to get a feel for the gods at their sacred places than it is from reading. If you do visit a site, what do you feel? Do you get any images or sensations? What does the place tell you?

If you are fortunate enough to have a museum in your city or town, another way to find out if a particular culture or pantheon sings to you is to visit displays of art of peoples of various cultures. Is there something familiar in any of the art? Does it speak to you in some way? That might be a clue to explore the mythology of the people who created it. It works the same way with music. Listen to music from cultures around the world, and see if any of it resonates with you. If it does, look into the mythology of that culture.

Yet another way to find your gods and goddesses is to shake your family tree, and explore the mythology of your family's country or culture of origin. If you're Irish or Scottish, the Celtic gods may resonate with you. If you're African American, you may choose to look into the deities of Africa. The gods of your bloodline may call to you.

To make things more complicated, sometimes—oftentimes, actually—a god or goddess will choose you instead of the other way around. This can be a profound and life-changing experience, and even a little scary at times. You'll know this is happening to you if you begin to encounter a lot of things or symbols associated with the deity in your regular life or in dreams and meditations. These symbols may pop up in conversation, on television, or other places. I know one Wiccan who started seeing owls everywhere she went. Within a short span of time, she saw a live one in a tree and images of them on jewelry, painted on a billboard, and even in an advertisement on the bus. She was thumbing through a magazine at the doctor's office and accidentally opened it to an article on owls. She was flipping channels and ran across a documentary on owls. She began to feel like she was being stalked by owls! She took the hint and looked into gods and goddesses associated with owls.

You may even see the deity who has chosen you in dreams. Sometimes they don't bother beating around the bush with subtle cues and simply make themselves known in showy, loud, hard-to-miss ways. They are the gods, after all.

Getting to Know Your Gods

The gods have favorite things, just like people do. As I already mentioned, they also have certain symbols and myths associated with them. Getting to know your deities means getting to know these preferences, symbols, and myths. Many gods are linked to certain animals, plants, colors, days of the week, seasons, incense, music, gestures, clothing, jewelry, stones, food, and much more. It's important to learn about these things in addition to reading the myths because it's the symbols and preferences that will make the gods feel welcome in your circle. If you are able to, consider learning a song from the god's country of origin to use in your ritual. You also may consider learning a few words of the language spoken by his or her original worshippers. If you can get inside the language of a people, you will begin to get an idea of how they think, and that can shed light on their concepts of deity. I learned some Irish in order to work with a Celtic goddess, and using just a few Irish words in that circle seemed to make the goddess energy more focused and palpable. I have seen a Mexican goddess invoked in a Yaqui sweat lodge in Spanish and Nahuatl with the same result. In addition to making the gods feel welcome, exploring each of these things puts you more in tune with them. If you can't find information on the items associated with a particular deity, try researching the culture the god came from instead. What can you find out about the people who worship(ped) this particular deity? What does that say about the deity? You can also take a pathworking journey to meet the god/dess and ask for more information.

Once you know what things are associated with the god/dess you are interested in working with, you can assemble some of them to use in ritual or to create an altar specifically for him or her. For example, the Norse goddess Freya is famous for her amber necklace, she is linked to cats and boars, and she is sometimes depicted wearing a helmet and breastplate. You can incorporate some of these things into your rite or altar setup or use them as inspiration for other symbols to include. Meditating in front of your special deity altar is a good way to tune in to the energy of the deity you've chosen, and it shows him or her that you are serious and respectful. There is more information on altars in chapter 8.

Four Points of Etiquette

There are four additional things you should know about working with the gods. First, although archetypes and "categories" of gods exist across the pantheons of the world, the gods are also products of the culture in which they are worshipped. In other words, most cultures have a mother goddess, but not all mother goddesses are the same, because the people who worship them are not the same. For example, the Egyptian goddess Sekhmet and the Celtic Morrigan are not the same simply because they're both "battle" goddesses associated with death and destruction. Each has her own separate stories, characteristics, and cultural context. To deny their unique origins is to treat them with disrespect. This is not a good idea; these are two goddesses I certainly would not want to tick off.

Second, and in a similar vein, it's important to learn all you can about the gods and their historic and mythological context and treat them accordingly rather than imposing your own ideas of what they are on them. I once had a woman try to convince me that the Indian goddess Kali was a loving mother goddess. Sure she is, in that "I'll stomp on your body, rip it to pieces, and drink your blood so your broken, tattered carcass can be enfolded in the bosom of mother earth and you can be reborn" sort of way. Although there is a mother aspect to Kali, she is not the same type of nurturing mother the woman in question was looking for.

That said, there are few historical records for some of the gods, so if you choose to work with the ones that are lesser known, you will have to extrapolate information about them from the sources you can find. Notice that I'm saying *extrapolate*, not *make up*. You can try pathworking to get more information about them too. It's not scholarly in the least, but it's better and more respectful than making something up to suit your purposes.

Third, and this is related to the second, if you are working with a god or gods that are not from your culture, be sure to examine what you are doing and make sure it is done with appreciation, not appropriation, of the other culture. Sometimes respecting another culture means leaving its gods alone because calling them into a Wiccan circle would not be appropriate. For example, I know Voodoo practitioners who think it's insulting for Wiccans to invoke the loa (Voodoo ancestral spirits) out of the context of Voodoo. Since Hinduism is still practiced actively by millions of people today, some Hindus believe it is inappropriate to invoke a Hindu deity into a Wiccan circle, since those deities have rites of their own that have been done for generations and fit into the Hindu cultural context.

Last, but not least, many Wiccans (but not all) consider it bad form to mix gods and goddesses from different pantheons in the same circle. For example, I would not call the Morrigan, Aries, and Sekhmet into the same ritual, and not just because of their temperaments. The words, gestures, and symbols that work for one would probably not work for the other two. Although they're all warriors, they don't speak the same language, whether literal or metaphorical. You can take the chance that they'll all sit around sharing war stories and comparing notches in their belts, but they might clash, and that's one catfight you do not want to be in the middle of. Similarly, don't call two gods or goddesses from the same pantheon who don't like each other into the same ritual. Do your research; the myths tend to be pretty clear about who gets along with whom.

As I mentioned earlier, Wiccans have a very personal relationship with their gods. Learning all of this stuff—their myths, cultures, and preferences—only helps deepen the relationship, which is rewarding in itself, but it also makes for better ritual and magic. Once you have chosen a particular god or goddess you would like to work with, and have studied him or her, you can use a variation of the "Introducing Yourself to the God and Goddess" ritual at the beginning of this chapter to introduce yourself. Just modify the exercise by incorporating some of the symbols of your chosen deity.

Calling the Gods into the Circle

There are two main reasons for calling the God and Goddess or another specific deity into a circle. You may ask them to be present for the ritual so you can honor, commune, and communicate with them, or you may ask them for something, such as guidance or help with a magical working. Or you can do both. Many Wiccans call the God and Goddess into every circle they perform simply to hang out with them and have them present—like family almost—for their rituals and workings. Others only call them for the eight Wiccan sabbats, or holidays (see chapter 9).

The God and Goddess are usually called once the circle is up and the quarters are called (if the quarters are going to be called). There is no set rule as to which you call first. Some Wiccans call the Goddess first because she gives birth to the universe. Others call the God first because he is the spark of life. Which you call first is entirely up to you.

Although in the "Introducing Yourself to the God and Goddess" ritual you lit a candle when you spoke to the God and Goddess, you do not have to do this every time. It is common, however, to have one candle for the God and one for the Goddess on the altar, and light each one in turn when you are calling them. For the purposes of the following example, we'll say that you do have candles, and that you're starting with the Goddess. We'll also say that you have an altar (see chapter 8). For the example, it can be simply a table with a tablecloth and the God and Goddess candles on it. The God candle should be red or gold, and the

Goddess candle should be white or silver. In this example, we'll also pretend that you're not going to be asking the God and Goddess for help with magical work.

1. Clean and clear your ritual space.

2. Ground.

3. Place your altar in what will be the center of your circle.

4. Cast your circle.

5. Call the quarters, if you'd like.

6. Stand before the altar, light the Goddess candle, and with your arms raised in a Y formation, palms facing forward, say something like:

    Great Goddess, Mother of All Things, Lady of the Moon, grace my ritual with your presence here tonight.

7. As you speak, feel the Goddess's presence fill the circle. Feel her energy flow into the sacred space. In your mind's eye, it might look like moonlight. Know that she is there. Do not pull her energy into your body.

8. Then light the God candle, put your hands in the Y position as before, and say something like:

    Great God, Father, Lord of the Sun, Lord of the Forest, Lord of the Hunt, grace my ritual with your presence here tonight.

9. As you speak, feel the God's presence fill the circle. Feel his energy flow into the sacred space. In your mind's eye, it might look like sunlight. Know that he is there. Do not pull his energy into your body.

10. At this point, you may wish to speak further to them, or, if it's a sabbat, you may do your sabbat rite (see chapter 9).

11. When your rite is concluded, stand in front of the altar again and say something like:

    Great God, thank you for blessing my ritual with your presence. Farewell.

12. Put out the God candle. Then say something like:

    Great Goddess, thank you for blessing my ritual with your presence. Farewell.

13. Put out the Goddess candle.

14. Dismiss the quarters if you called them, draw up your circle, and ground.

You can modify this simple formula for a circle that includes magic. You might change the invocations and farewells to something like:

> *Great Goddess, Mother of All Things, Lady of the Moon, grace my ritual with your presence here tonight and assist me with my healing (or other type of) spell.*

Great Goddess, thank you for blessing my ritual and my healing (or other type of) magic with your presence. Hail, and farewell.

Great God, Father, Lord of the Sun, Lord of the Forest, Lord of the Hunt, grace my ritual with your presence here tonight and assist me with my healing (or other type of) spell.

Great God, thank you for blessing my ritual and my healing (or other type of) magic with your presence. Hail, and farewell.

You can be a lot more poetic than I am being here. These bare-bones examples are just to get you started. If you are working with a specific god or goddess, you can (and should) also tailor the calls to him or her. For example:

Great Mother Isis, Goddess of the Earth, Protector of the Dead, be here tonight to bless my ritual and magic.

Lord Apollo, God of Light, God of Music, God of Prophesy, lend your great power to my ritual and magic tonight.

Cerridwen, shape-changing goddess, Patroness of Poets, shine your bright inspiration on my ritual and magic.

Thor, God of Thunder and Lightning, God of the Sky, protect and bless this circle and all within it.

If you do your homework and truly get to know your gods, the invocations will flow easily for you. As long as they are sincere and from the heart, they will be heard.

8

Tools, Toys, and Altars

So far, we've talked about building a ritual circle, calling the quarters, and calling the gods. As I said earlier on, it's important to be able to do these things without ritual tools because ultimately the tools are just props, and the Wiccan is the real force behind building the circle; the real will behind channeling the earth energy. I placed this chapter after those others because it's easy for beginning Wiccans to be distracted by the tools (aka toys) and lose their focus on what's really important—their own spiritual and psychic development. A bright, shiny set of tools is no replacement for actually doing the mental and energetic work of Wicca.

Then why do Wiccans use tools? A Wiccan's magical tools are like extensions of him- or herself. They are infused with their owner's energy and attuned toward his or her will.

They enhance ritual and magic by helping their owner focus energy. In addition, since the tools are only used in ritual or magic, and since each one has deep symbolic meaning, simply picking them up helps their owner get into the ritual mindset.

Wiccan ritual tools need not be expensive or fancy, but they should be special and have significance to their owner. Oral lore from some Wiccan traditions states that the Wiccan should make the tools him- or herself. Since we're not all blacksmiths or woodcarvers, this isn't practical, but if you can make or modify any of your own tools, they will be more a part of you than if you purchase them.

The Primary Wiccan Tools

Here is a rundown of the main Wiccan tools. There are some additional tools that are specific to certain Wiccan traditions, but since this book is about Wicca in general, we'll stick to the basics.

Athame

The athame is the Wiccan's most important tool. It is a double-edged ritual knife, often, but not always, with a black handle. The two sides symbolize the God and the Goddess, who come together at the point; the union of the spiritual and the mundane worlds; and the idea that with power comes responsibility. The athame may or may not be sharp, depending on the preference of the owner. It is never used to cut anything but energy and air. Some traditions hold that if the athame ever draws blood, it must be destroyed, but this is by no means a universal Wiccan belief. Nevertheless, if you're prone to dropping things on your feet, you may want an athame that isn't too sharp. Its sharpness has nothing to do with how it works as a magical tool.

The athame is used to focus and direct energy, especially when drawing the circle or calling the quarters. It is associated most commonly with the element of air and the east quarter, but some associate it with fire and the south. It symbolizes the Wiccan's will. Members of a coven or group can share many of the other tools, but the athame is always personal. Do not touch another person's athame (or other ritual tools, for that matter) without permission.

If you hang out with Wiccans, you will hear the word "athame" pronounced about ten different ways, so don't worry about getting it right. Some of the most popular are a-THAH-may, ah-THAH-me, ah-THAW-may, and ATH-um-ay. Give it your best shot.

Wand

The wand is simply a fancy stick. You may think I'm being irreverent, but the traditional wand is a piece of slender branch cut to a certain length, usually at least a foot long. Which is a nice way of saying it's a stick. The length varies by tradition, so you can cut yours as long or as short as you wish. It may or may not be stripped of bark. Some Wiccans carve magical symbols into their wands. The type of wood varies by tradition too. Common woods for Wiccan wands are oak, ash, and willow. You should take the wood from a fallen branch rather than cutting it from a live tree. Some Wiccans like to "thank" the tree that provided the branch by leaving an offering of water or compost at its base.

You can make a wand from a thick dowel purchased at a hardware store, but in my (very biased) opinion, it's more "organic," for lack of a better word, to use a bit of branch. If you go to eBay or anywhere online that sells wands, you will find a wide variety made of all sorts of things, like copper, crystals, antlers, bone, silver, and steel. Although they're not wood, any of these will work if you think they will. The important part is how the wand resonates with its owner.

Like the athame, the wand is used to focus energy. It is most often used when invoking the gods, since it's not polite or smart to wave a sharp, pointy athame at Athena or Loki. It can also be used to call the quarters and draw the circle. It's used especially in rituals that invoke the Horned God or involve phallic symbolism. Sometimes, the wand is carved to look like a phallus. The wand is most often associated with fire and the south, but some Wiccans link it to air and the east.

Chalice

The chalice represents the Goddess and the womb. It is used to drink from, especially in rituals where feminine symbolism is important. There is a ritual that is common in Wiccan circles where the blade of the athame is lowered into the chalice to symbolize the sexual union of the God and Goddess. The chalice can be made of nearly anything—

glass, ceramic, wood, metal—but I don't recommend plastic. The "loaner" cup for people in our training circle who forget theirs is plastic, and it just feels wrong. If you choose metal, make sure it's a metal that you can drink from safely. If you're a little accident-prone, try to find a wooden chalice. I know one high priest who is notorious for knocking over and shattering ceramic chalices, and we have more than one super-glued ritual cup in our cupboard. Often you can find great chalices at art fairs and thrift stores. The chalice is associated with water and the west.

Cauldron

The cauldron is a big cast-iron pot on three feet. It is used to represent feminine energy, like the chalice. It is also used to burn things in or build "bonfires." (Fill the cauldron about half full of clean clay kitty litter, stick candles in the litter, and light them. Have a fire extinguisher handy and be careful! Do this outside.) Although Shakespeare would have you believe that witches and Wiccans boil brews in their cauldrons, this is not true for the most part. They usually use the stove like everyone else. You can find small cauldrons at many occult and metaphysical shops and Web sites. Other places to look are antique shops and flea markets, especially ones that are held in rural areas. The cauldron is associated with water and the west.

Broom

A Wiccan ritual broom can be an ordinary broom, a handmade one, or a decorative one like those found in craft stores. The bristles represent a woman's pubic area and the handle represents a phallus, so the broom is a symbol of the sexual union of the God and Goddess. It is used to sweep energy out of the circle space before drawing the circle. Some Wiccans also use the broom to raise energy in circle. The broom is associated with either earth and the north or air and the east.

Censer and Incense

Wiccans frequently burn incense in their ritual circles to set the mood and attract the kinds of energy they need for their rituals. All herbs and scents have magical correspondences. Wiccans also use incense to purify the ritual space and consecrate items for ritual use by passing them through the smoke. You can use any type of incense and censer in a Wiccan ritual. Most of the Wiccans I know use the loose incense that you burn on charcoal, but you can use sticks or cones too. The advantage of the loose stuff is that you can blend your own herbs or buy a special blend that suits your purposes. If you think you might like to try making your own incense, read up on each herb before you include it. Some of them are toxic when inhaled. The censer and incense represent fire and air, south and east.

Salt and Water

Many Wiccans keep a dish of salt and a dish of water on their altars. Most often, some of the salt is mixed into the water, and the saltwater is used to bless and purify the ritual circle. It can also be used to consecrate items for ritual use.

In a pinch, the water is also helpful if you have an accident with the incense or the candles. Salt and water are associated with earth and water, north and west.

Candles

Wiccans go through a lot of candles. I have never been to a Wiccan ritual that didn't include them. As I said previously, Wiccans may place candles on the altar to represent the God and Goddess. Candles are used for reading light and to mark the quarters. Sometimes they just serve to set the mood. They are used commonly in magic. Choose a color that corresponds with your magical or ritual purpose. You can find information about color correspondences in several of the books on the recommended reading list. You can use any type of candle you wish. Seven-day candles, like those found in Christian stores, occult stores, botanicas, or the Mexican food section of some grocery stores, are great because they are candle and holder in one, and they're not as easy to knock over as tapers. One of my coveners has a talent for finding whole boxes of unused tapers at garage sales. Whatever type of candle you choose, make sure to use a sturdy holder and keep a fire extinguisher nearby. Watch your hair and sleeves around the candles too! I've been in two separate rituals where a woman's hair caught fire and she didn't know she was burning until people started smacking her to put it out. I've also been in a skyclad (naked) ritual where someone accidentally put out the God candle with his bare backside. He has never lived this down, of course. Candles, naturally, represent fire and the south.

Utility Knife

Since you can't cut anything solid with your athame, it's handy to have a ritual utility knife for cutting herbs, cord, or anything else you might need in ritual or magic, or for carving symbols into candles and wands. The utility knife can be any kind of knife, but it should be set aside specifically for ritual and magical use.

Statues

Wiccans often use statues on their altars to represent the God and Goddess. This is not essential, but it adds to the spiritual atmosphere. You can find great statues online or at occult or metaphysical stores. Sacred Source, www.sacredsource.com, has an amazing selection.

Book of Shadows

The book of shadows, often referred to affectionately as the BOS, is a combination spell book and magical diary. Wiccans use them to record rituals and spells they wrote and whether or not they were successful. The BOS can be anything from a three-ring notebook to a bound blank book that you write in. Some Wiccans draw gorgeous borders on the pages of their books, like medieval manuscripts. Other books are very plain. You can keep your BOS on your hard drive, but it's kind of hard to lug your computer into circle. If you go online, particularly to eBay, you will find people selling "books of shadows." Most of the time these are either plagiarized or not genuine, and the people selling them are only interested in squeezing as much money from you as they can. The best books of shadows are either inherited through your tradition, if you have one, or created by you, or both. As you explore your path and find or write techniques and rituals that work for you, your book will grow.

This list of tools is not exhaustive, but it covers the basics. Acquire your tools slowly over time rather than rushing out to get them all at once. That way, you'll have time to find or make the ones that resonate with you most.

Wiccan Altars

Wiccans seem to love their altars. Whether it's because of their devotion to the gods or their devotion to knickknacks (or both) we'll never know, but either way, altars are a place for Wiccans to express their faith, do their spiritual work, store their ritual paraphernalia, and/or channel their inner Martha Stewart or Christopher Lowell. A Wiccan altar can be as simple as a small shelf with a pine cone and a candle on it or as elaborate as a full table with a cloth, candles, incense, flowers, ritual tools, and statues. Wiccans use altars as decorative and devotional spaces around their homes and gardens and also in ritual. For the purposes of this chapter, a devotional altar is one that is set up permanently in the home or garden, and a ritual altar is one that is used only in a particular ritual circle.

The Surface

There are no rules about how big, small, fancy, or simple a Wiccan altar has to be, so you can create one out of whatever suits you and speaks to you. I have seen altars made on end tables, coffee tables, shelves, file cabinets, sewing tables, dresser and desktops, milk boxes, boards, flat rocks, small mounds of soil, garden stepping stones, TV trays, fireplace mantels, old trunks, cedar chests, plate rails, refrigerator tops, wall nooks, and even an old tombstone. (The tombstone had a typo in it, so it had never been used to mark a grave.) If you are creating a devotional altar, it's best if you can find a small table or use the top of a bookcase, but if you don't have the cash or space for these, that's okay. You can use any flat surface if you need to, assuming it's easy to clean and meditate in front of. If you do have a few extra dollars, consider scrounging around thrift stores for an old end table. These tend to be reasonably inexpensive. If the one you find is ugly (and they often are, or they wouldn't have been relegated to the store), you can paint it or cover it with an inexpensive cloth. If you have pets and you are creating a devotional altar, you will also want to consider what we call the "cat factor." Cats (and some dogs and most parrots) are irresistibly drawn to unsteady surfaces full of fragile knickknacks. If you have a curious feline or canine in the house, consider building your devotional altar either up high or on a very stable surface, preferably both. (The TV tray is not recommended for this situation!)

If you are creating a ritual altar, you will want something that can be taken down and stowed or put aside when it's not in use. I've found that trunks and chests are great for this because you can store your ritual tools inside and use the surface for the altar during ritual. It's also perfectly okay to use an everyday table or surface in ritual. I know plenty of Wiccans who move their coffee tables into their circle space for ritual and put them back in the living room when they're done. Stability is important for a ritual altar too, especially if you will be moving around it or you will have burning candles on it.

Covering and Paraphernalia

Once you have found a surface, decide if you would like to cover it. Most Wiccan altars have altar cloths of some kind, but I've also seen altars that have been painted with magical symbols, stars and moons, or spirals. If you want to use a cloth, you can buy a new tablecloth, find used ones at thrift stores or garage sales (or in your own drawers), use extra pieces of fabric left over from sewing projects or bought new, or use scarves or sarongs. You could even use your grandmother's lace doilies, as long as you're not building an altar to a deity like Thor or Aries. Whether you're creating a devotional or ritual altar, you can change the cloths to reflect the current season or sabbat, using different colors and textures for each time of year.

So now that you have this great surface, what do you put on it? Again, there are no hard and fast rules, but Wiccan altars often have candles, statues, flowers, stones, feathers, shells, incense and incense burners, and/or the Wiccan's ritual tools on them. Sometimes they include foods or beverages associated with a particular sabbat or deity. Remember to change these periodically if they're not in some sort of packaging,

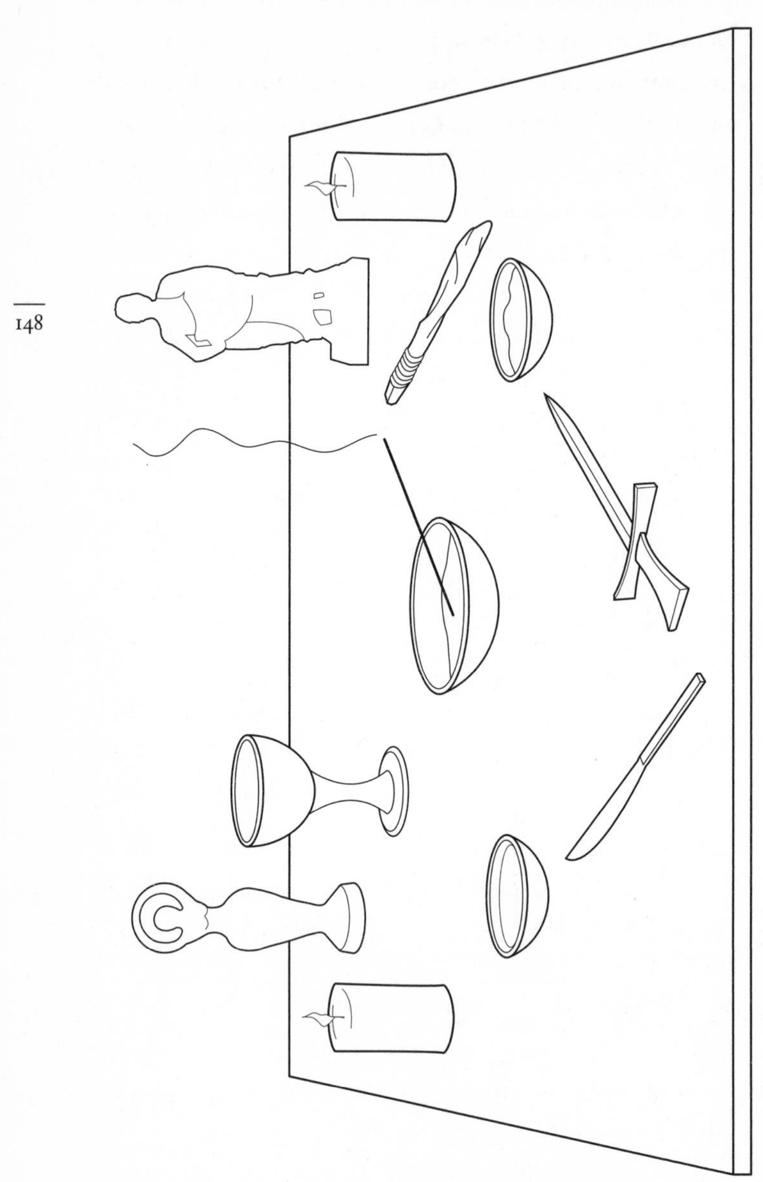

Sample Altar Setup

lest they increase the cat factor, bug factor, or slimy-mold factor.

As I mentioned in chapter 7, if you're building a devotional altar to a specific deity, you'll want to find items that correspond to him or her. For example, I have an altar for the Morrigan, a Celtic warrior goddess. The surface is covered with a red cloth, and on it are a candle in a red, cauldron-shaped holder; a statue of the Morrigan; the skull, feathers, and feet of a crow; a raven figurine; a coin with a wolf on it; my raven bracelet; and my cherry-amber ritual necklace. Wolves, crows, and ravens are the Morrigan's animals, and since she's a battle goddess, I figure she likes red. I didn't include any flowers because the Morrigan isn't a flowery kind of girl.

Ritual altars often have decorative items on them, such as Indian corn at the Fall Equinox, but it's more important that they contain the tools and materials necessary for the ritual itself. Often, these items are put on the altar in symbolic places, for example, the censer at the south edge of the altar because of its association with fire. However, sometimes it's much more important to have the items laid out so they're easy to grab and use than it is to have them in special places. There is no right or wrong way to set up a ritual altar. The diagram here shows a sample altar setup. Feel free to use it as is, adapt it in whatever way suits you, or throw it out entirely.

In this altar design, the altar is facing north. This is common in Wicca, although altars sometimes face one of the other directions. I put the athame on the right because I am right-handed and it's easier to grab there, and since the athame is used a lot in circle, I want it handy. The utility knife is on the left to balance the athame. The censer is in the middle so it's less likely to be tipped over. The god candle and statue are on the right because the God is the active principle and, as I mentioned earlier, the right hand is considered by some to be the active hand. The goddess statue and candle are on the left because the Goddess is the receptive principle. The water and salt are in the west and east purely for aesthetic balance. Water is west, but salt (earth) isn't east (it's north). I put the chalice by the goddess statue and candle because it symbolizes her; likewise for the wand and the god statue and candle. The broom doesn't go on the altar.

Remember, you don't need all of this stuff to do effective ritual! Also, if you are a minimalist who abhors clutter, you don't have to put every tool on the altar. Most people don't use every tool in every ritual anyway.

Consecrating Tools

Most Wiccans consecrate each of their tools before they use them in ritual. "Consecrate" means to make something sacred or devote it to a deity or to spiritual use. When you consecrate your tools, you are saying, more or less, "I'm dedicating these tools to my gods, my spiritual path, and working my will." If you choose to consecrate your tools, you only need to consecrate everything once—not for every circle. The following is an example of a tool-consecration ritual. As with all of the exercises and rituals in this book, modify it to suit your needs.

You will need:

- A bowl of salt and one of water. There should be only about a tablespoon of salt, but the water bowl should be about half full. Do not overfill it.
- Your censer and incense, unlit, plus matches or a lighter.
- Athame.
- All of your other ritual tools. Don't worry if you don't have all of them yet. You don't have to consecrate them all at once. It makes for a very long ritual if you do.
- A clean, dry rag or towel.

Ritual Instructions

1. Place your altar in the center of your circle space. Put the water, salt, and all of your tools either alongside or under it. You may wish to have one burning candle on the altar for light.
2. Ground.
3. Clear the space through visualization rather than by using the broom.
4. Draw the circle using your fingers and not the athame or wand.
5. Call the quarters, again using your fingers and not the athame or wand.

6. Call the God and Goddess.
7. Stand or sit in front of your altar. Put both hands on the surface and draw up some earth energy through your taproot. Say something like:

   I bless and consecrate this altar in the names of the Goddess and God and in the presence of the powers of the four elements. May it aid me in honoring my gods and working my will. Blessed be.

8. As you say this, visualize the earth energy flowing from your hands and filling the altar, infusing it with power and pushing out any unwanted or negative energy that might be in it. Tables don't tend to harbor negative energy (why would it hang out in a table?), but it doesn't hurt to push out the vibes of its previous owner, if it had one.
9. Next, place the bowls of salt and water on the altar. Place your index and middle fingers in the water and say something like:

   I bless and consecrate this water and bowl in the names of the Goddess and God and in the presence of the powers of the four elements. May it aid me in honoring my gods and working my will. Blessed be.

10. As you are saying this, raise earth energy through your taproot and infuse and energize the water and bowl with it.

11. Repeat the same procedure with the salt, then pour the salt into the water and stir with your two fingers.

12. Next, place the censer and incense on the altar, and repeat the blessing on each one. Then put some incense in the censer and light it.

13. It is traditional when consecrating tools to expose them to all four elements. The four elements are represented in the incense and saltwater. Sprinkle the altar and censer lightly with the saltwater (don't put out the incense!), then pick up the censer (if it's heatproof and safe) and fan the smoke over the altar and bowls. Now everything on the altar has been blessed by the elements.

14. Next, pick up your athame. Raise earth energy from your taproot and say something like:

    I bless and consecrate this athame in the names of the Goddess and God and in the presence of the powers of the four elements. May it aid me in honoring my gods and working my will. Blessed be.

15. Sprinkle the athame with the saltwater and hold it in the incense smoke for a moment. *Then wipe the saltwater off of your blade with the rag.* You will not wipe it off of anything else except the utility knife, but you don't want saltwater sitting on your athame or you'll end up with rust or pits in the blade. You'll also want

to polish the blade later with Metal Glo or some similar product. Real Wiccans know how to take care of their blades! The athame is your most personal tool, so treat it with extra respect.

16. Repeat this procedure with your other tools, but instead of holding the tool or pointing at it with your fingers, direct the earth energy through your athame toward the tool. Sprinkle and cense each tool. You do not have to consecrate every candle or batch of incense you use unless you want to, but it's a good idea to do the candle holders.
17. When you have finished, thank the God and Goddess for attending your ritual.
18. Dismiss the quarters.
19. Take up the circle.
20. Ground.
21. Store your newly consecrated tools in a safe, special place.

9

Wiccan Holidays and the Wheel of the Year

WICCANS CELEBRATE HOLIDAYS (called sabbats) and the full moons. Since Wicca is a nature-oriented religion, it places great emphasis on the changing cycle of the seasons, which Wiccans refer to as the "wheel of the year." The Wiccan wheel has eight "spokes" on it, each representing a sabbat and marking an important point in the turning of the year and the movement of the earth around the sun. The sabbats fall about six weeks apart. Four of them occur at the solstice and equinox points. The other four, sometimes referred to as the "cross quarters," fall midway between the solstices and equinoxes.

In addition to marking the seasons, the Wiccan sabbats tell the stories of the God and Goddess and celebrate Wiccans' connections to the spiritual world. As I mentioned in the early chapters of this book, Wiccans are concerned with both the spiritual world and the "here and now." In their sabbats, they often reenact what is happening in nature in order to engage fully with the world around them and participate in the turning of the wheel. They also use these times to connect and identify with their gods.

Many Wiccans refer to full moon rituals as "esbats." At the full moon, the moon (the Goddess) is opposite the sun (the God) in the heavens, with the earth in between like a child in the embrace of its parents. Astrology tells us that the full moon is the time of culmination. This has long been believed to be a time of great magical power, when the Goddess is in her full glory, and so Wiccans will often, but not always, honor the Goddess over the God at the full moon. Don't worry, though—the God gets his due at the sabbats, and just because others focus on the Goddess doesn't mean you have to. Because the full moon is so powerful, Wiccans will often do magic during their esbats in addition to honoring the gods. Some Wiccans use the same ritual for every full moon, and others write new ones. There is no consistent, agreed-on way to celebrate the full moons or symbol set for each one. Wiccans mark those days however the moon moves them to. This does not mean that the full moons aren't important. In fact, in some traditions they are considered more core to Wiccan practice than the sabbats.

Each sabbat does have its own set of symbols, images, and myths. There is no one right way to celebrate each sabbat, and different Wiccans interpret the meanings differently, so I am going to give you some background information on each that you can use as a starting point to create your own meaningful seasonal rituals.

February 2: Imbolc, Oimelc, Candlemas

Imbolc celebrates the first stirrings of life under the blanket of winter. The light begins to grow noticeably. The land is becoming fertile and ripe for new growth, and like it, we are getting ready for the coming spring and our spiritual rebirth after the inner work of winter. The Goddess gave birth to the God at the Winter Solstice, and as his strength grows at Imbolc, she prepares for the cycle of life, death, and rebirth to begin all over again.

Some themes for Imbolc are fertility, fire, purification, and initiation or spiritual rebirth. If you live in the north, the idea that this is a fertility festival may be a bit of a reach for you, but if you live in a moderate climate, the buds on the trees this time of year might serve as a reminder. Perhaps it is better to think of it as the potential for fertility; the moment when the earth ceases to be lifeless and begins to awaken.

Fire, of course, symbolizes the warming of the earth, the spark of life, and the coming of the light. Many sabbats feature fire in one way or another, but at Imbolc, Wiccans speak of the "fire within" rather than literal fire. Wiccan Imbolc ceremonies tend to include lots of candles to encourage the light and warmth to grow. The Irish goddess/saint Brid, whose feast day is February 2, is often associated with fire. She is a goddess of the forge, so this is no surprise. She is also a goddess of inspiration, poetry, and fertility, so she embodies several Imbolc themes. Many Wiccans honor Brid at Imbolc.

This is also a time of purification, in the sense of sloughing off the darkness of winter and getting rid of extraneous stuff that keeps you from your spiritual potential. The connection between fertility, purification, and spiritual rebirth is echoed in the name "February." In ancient Rome, the people sacrificed a goat in honor of Juno, mother of the gods; cut the goat skin into strips called *februa*, which meant "instruments of purification" (and which comes from the same root as "February"); and ceremonially smacked the strips across the backside of each woman, simultaneously honoring the mother goddess and ensuring their fertility. Remnants of this ritual, which was associated with the festival of Lupercalia, still exist today.

Perhaps because of the season's association with spiritual rebirth, many Wiccans do dedications or initiations at this time of year. Dedications are simple ceremonies, either public or private, where a person declares his or her intent to study Wicca and/or honor the gods. An initiation ceremony is when a person is "made" a Wiccan—he or she ceases to be a dedicant and is now truly walking the Wiccan path. Initiation often includes joining a Wiccan group or tradition, although many Wiccans work alone. Initiation is considered a birth or rebirth, and, like in an Imbolc circle, the underlying feelings in an initiation ceremony are often anticipation and newness.

When you are studying a sabbat, it is important also to study the sabbat opposite it on the wheel of the year and the relationship between the two holidays. Opposite sabbats form yet another Wiccan polarity. Imbolc is opposite Lammas, August 1. Decorations for a seasonal Imbolc altar might include bulbs and seeds and lots of candles.

March 21: Spring Equinox, Ostara

At the Spring Equinox, Wiccans celebrate, well—spring! The potential of Imbolc is beginning to become reality as tulips and daffodils pop up, people sow first seeds, and darkness turns toward light. Daytime and nighttime are equal, so balance is emphasized. There is a sexual spark in the air too and new life busting out everywhere.

In some ways, the Wiccan Spring Equinox is like Easter. On the secular side of Easter, people celebrate with colored eggs and chocolate rabbits. There are few things you can have on the table in mixed company that symbolize fertility (sex) and new life more than eggs and those rather prolific rabbits, and as if that wasn't good enough, Easter also comes with a rabbit that delivers eggs. On the religious side, Christians celebrate Easter as the day when Jesus conquers death and rises from the tomb. In the Northern Hemisphere, the Spring Equinox is when the sun rises over the horizon, and light vanquishes darkness. The Wiccan God is rising and coming into his power too.

It is common to have lots of flowers at a Wiccan Spring Equinox circle. This is partly because they're beautiful and available and everything is blooming around us, but, as any Georgia O'Keefe fan will tell you, flowers, like those eggs and rabbits, are symbols of sex and fertility, so there is more than one reason they're included.

The balance of light and darkness is important at the Spring and Fall Equinoxes. At these times, Wiccans are keenly aware of the polarity of darkness and light and the importance of one to the other. Lots of spiritual people, both Wiccan and non-Wiccan, see religion as a way to seek balance in their lives. Balance between work and play, ego and humility, compassion and strength, heaven and earth. However, the two equinoxes also point out to us how abnormal balance is. We pay balance a lot of lip service as one of the goals of our life quest. We may see a therapist, take a retreat, use drugs and alcohol, join a support group, and do endless other things to try to achieve it. Yet, the equinoxes remind us, day and night are only balanced two days a year. The state of balance, although desirable, is not common. Naturally, the two days when the world seems to be in balance are days of great power. And although the Spring Equinox sits at the point of balance, we can feel the energy turning toward the light.

There is a playfulness to the Spring Equinox. Some Wiccans see the Wiccan Goddess as a maiden and the God as a growing adolescent at this sabbat. The hard work of the winter is done, and the harvest is yet to come, so it's time to relax and enjoy the beautiful world blooming all around us.

As you have probably guessed, the sabbat opposite the Spring Equinox is the Fall Equinox, September 21. Decorations for a seasonal Spring Equinox altar might include flowers, eggs, seeds, and images of rabbits.

May 1: Beltane

At Beltane, many Wiccans celebrate the sexual union of the God and Goddess and what it will yield: fertile fields, the harvest, sustenance for another year, and a new cycle of life. On Beltane in parts of Europe in centuries past, young women would go "a-Maying" all night in the woods with their lovers, and many would come back pregnant. They might also "bless" the tilled fields by making love in the furrows. There is nothing subtle about Beltane; despite its trappings of fun and games, it's not a G-rated holiday.

Perhaps the best-known symbol of Beltane, or May Day, is the Maypole. The top of the Maypole pierces a garland of flowers, from which fall colored ribbons. Men and women, divided by gender into two concentric circles, dance around the pole in opposite directions while holding the ends of the ribbons, weaving in and out between each other until the pole is completely bound. The symbolism is obvious.

The fairy court is said to move twice a year, and some Wiccans believe that Beltane is one of those times. Wiccans who work with the fey might leave out libations such as cake or a saucer of milk to honor the "fair folk" and appease them so they don't play tricks.

At Beltane, the God is often portrayed as the Green Man —a man completely dressed or covered in foliage. The Green Man is lord of the forest and growing things—the essence of plant life. There is a wild, feral, unpredictable side to him, but he has a gentle side too. If you feel like wandering in the woods under the moon at Beltane, you might be in tune with the Green Man. Just be careful, because even the Green Man can trip over a root or conk his head on a low branch in the dark.

Where the atmosphere of the Spring Equinox is playful, Beltane is joyous. The God and the Goddess are mature, strong, and in love. There is often a lot of feasting at Beltane celebrations, and some Wiccans include beer because it is made of John Barleycorn, the grain, associated with the Green Man. Wiccan Beltane rites, like Spring Equinox ones, are full of flowers and greenery, and women and sometimes men will wear garlands on their heads. Like Imbolc, Beltane is a fire festival, and outdoor Wiccan ceremonies will often include a bonfire. Couples take hands and jump over the fire together to increase their fertility. If you do this, keep a fire extinguisher handy, build a small bonfire, don't wear anything that will drag in the flames, and be careful! The rites may also contain symbolic sex rituals, and it is not uncommon for established couples to sneak off and go a-Maying after the circle is over. It goes without saying that magic to conceive a child is often done at Beltane.

The sabbat opposite Beltane is Samhain or Halloween, October 31. Decorations for a seasonal Beltane altar might include flowers, greenery, ribbons, and phallic symbols.

June 21:
Summer Solstice, Midsummer, Litha

The Summer Solstice is the longest day of the year in the Northern Hemisphere, and the sun is at its full power. At the Summer Solstice, some Wiccans believe the God is in his full glory and the Goddess is pregnant both with child and with the harvest. Other Wiccans celebrate the Summer Solstice as the day when the dark half of the year conquers the light half. This is sometimes symbolized as a battle between two kings: the Oak King and the Holly King.

The Oak King/Holly King idea may have been pieced together from fragments of old European tradition. The Summer Solstice was a fire festival in much of old Europe—the last hurrah before the days began to shorten again. One custom was to light barrels and roll them down hills to represent the sun. In French ceremonies, men chosen as "kings" gave up their crowns and pretended to die, representing the light giving way to darkness and the turning of the year. Legend has it that King Louis XIV—called the "Sun King" because of his riches and because he self-identified with the Greek sun god Apollo—was the last real French king to participate in this rite. According to Sir James Frazer in *The Golden Bough*:

> The French kings often witnessed these spectacles and even lit the bonfire with their own hands. In 1648 Louis the Fourteenth, crowned with a wreath of roses and carrying a bunch of roses in his hand, kindled the fire, danced

> at it and partook of the banquet afterwards in the town hall. But this was the last occasion when a monarch presided at the midsummer bonfire in Paris.[1]

Frazer, however, believed that Midsummer/Summer Solstice bonfires were not about kings but rather for protection against witches. A different legend has it that Louis banned Midsummer fires.

Whether the God gives way or maintains his position, at the Summer Solstice he stands at his highest point, and from there he can look backward at the months that have passed and forward to what will come. Because of this, some Wiccans believe that divination is especially effective at this solstice.

Like Beltane, the Summer Solstice is said to be one of the times of the year when the fairy court changes residence. Anyone who has ever seen fireflies flitting around on Midsummer night might believe this is true, and certainly Shakespeare thought there was enough connection between the fey and Midsummer to write an entire play about it.

Although they acknowledge the pregnant Goddess, Wiccan Summer Solstice rites tend to be geared toward the God. They usually include bonfires, even if they have to be tiny, contained, indoor ones, but if the Wiccans have the luxury of outdoor space and privacy, often they will dance around the fire. The mood of a Wiccan Midsummer right is like a raucous party tinged with the awareness that tomorrow is a

1. Sir James Frazer, *The Golden Bough* (1922; reprint, London: Penguin Books, 1996).

darker, more serious day. Like Shakespeare's fairy glamour, it brings a sense of gleeful but fleeting revelry.

The sabbat opposite the Summer Solstice is Yule—the Winter Solstice—December 21. Decorations for a seasonal Summer Solstice altar might include oak leaves, symbols of the sun, and flowers, especially roses or sunflowers.

August 1: Lammas, Lughnasadh

Wiccans sometimes refer to Lammas, or Lughnasadh, as the first of the three harvest festivals. In the Northern Hemisphere, at Lammas the first grains and fruits are harvested. Grain—wheat, corn, and barley—is one of the main symbols of this holiday. Wiccans give thanks for the bounty of the earth. Another important theme of this holiday is sacrifice; not human or animal sacrifice (remember, Wiccans don't do either of these things!), but the knowledge that there is a price for everything, and one thing must be given up to allow for the birth of another.

The word Lammas is thought to be a corruption of the phrase "Loaf Mass," which was a European celebration where bread was baked from the first crop of wheat. Wheat or grain is thought to be a symbol of the God, and some Wiccans mark Lammas as the death of the God; the time when he gives up his life force to sustain humanity and begins to descend to the underworld, from where he will later be reborn.

There are several legends about the European "sacred king" or "divine king" associated with this holiday. The basic idea is that "the king and the land are one." The king is the representative of the people and the God, and the land is the Goddess. At Beltane, they join in order to create the fruits of the harvest, and at Lammas, the king/God dies in order to feed the people and start the cycle of rebirth.

It is an old idea that in times of famine, the king, as the people's emissary, would be sacrificed in order to bring about the harvest. After all, if you want to appease the powers of nature, you don't give up a weak person, you give up the strongest. Sometimes, if it was impossible or impractical to sacrifice the king, a noble man would be offered as a surrogate. As I mentioned in chapter 1, Dr. Margaret Murray and others, including Gerald Gardner, hypothesized that this legend has been played out over and over again by real kings in British history. They thought that royal blood had been spilled to defend England against the Spanish Armada and that Thomas à Becket had been a surrogate for a sacred king. In one of his books, Gardner even writes about England's witches gathering for a huge ritual during World War II to repel Hitler. In his account, they magically sent Hitler the message "You can not come," and they expended so much energy in the ritual that some of the older witches died as a result. There is a novel called *Lammas Night* by Katherine Kurtz that contains a fanciful "history" about the British divine king, and the cheesy-but-great Wiccan must-see movie *The Wicker Man* (1973) covers some of the same territory, although inexplicably it is set at Beltane instead of Lammas. (If you rent this, get the British version and not the chopped-up American version edited by Roger Corman.)

Whether this sacred king stuff is true is more than questionable, and Gardner and Murray have been criticized endlessly for propagating it. Nevertheless, it is woven into the folklore and symbolism of Lammas. At Lammas, and at Loaf Mass, bread was sometimes baked into the shape of a man and torn apart to symbolize the sacrifice of the divine sacred king or his surrogate. Some Wiccans carry on this tradition in their Lammas rituals. Others prefer the symbolism of John Barleycorn. There are several old folk songs personifying the barley as John Barleycorn and honoring his demise and rebirth as beer. Certainly, beer is more fun at a Lammas sabbat than a loaf of bread.

The other common Wiccan name for this sabbat, Lughnasadh, means something like "the games of Lugh" or "the festival of Lugh." Lugh was the Celtic god of light and the sun, and he carried a magic spear. Competition and games, both associated with Lugh, are common at this sabbat.

Lammas is generally a happy sabbat, but it is tinged with the knowledge of death and the coming darkness. What we enjoy at the harvest comes at a price; the death of the seed means life for all of us. All of the sabbats mark changing points in the year, but transformation is highlighted at Lammas.

Lammas is opposite Imbolc on the wheel of the year. At Imbolc, Wiccans celebrate the potential of the light and the God, and at Lammas they enjoy the fruits of that potential.

Decorations for a seasonal Lammas altar might include bread, wheat or wheat weavings, beer, or a sickle.

September 21: Fall Equinox, Mabon

Many Wiccans celebrate the Fall Equinox as the second of three harvests. The sense of winter approaching is keener, and once again day and night are equal, but this time light is giving way to darkness.

Mabon is the Welsh god of music, sometimes called "the divine youth," and there is a lot of speculation about how his name became associated with this sabbat. Personally, I do not know what the real answer to that is, but I have included the name here because if you hang out with Wiccans long enough, you're bound to hear it.

Some Wiccans celebrate the Fall Equinox as the time when either the Goddess or the God descends to the underworld. There are many underworld myths and legends from around the world. One of the most famous is the Greek story of Demeter and her daughter Persephone. There are many variations on this myth, but the gist of it is that Hades, god of the underworld, abducts Persephone to be his queen, and Demeter, goddess of the grain, blights the earth and will not allow anything to grow until Persephone is returned to her. But while she is in the underworld, Persephone eats some pomegranate seeds. Whoever eats anything in the underworld has to stay there (this goes for the fairy realms too, in case you ever find yourself there), but because the world is suffering under the blight, the gods work out a deal where Persephone will stay in the underworld for either three or six months (one for each seed she ate) and return to earth for the remainder of the year. When Persephone returns to earth, she has changed because she has experienced death, so Wiccans see her as a symbol of transformation and wisdom. Many Wiccans include pomegranates in their Fall Equinox ceremonies in honor of Persephone.

One of the aspects of the Wiccan God is that he is the king of the dead, and at this holiday some Wiccans believe he takes up that crown. Others believe he does so at Lammas or Samhain.

Still others mark the Fall Equinox with festivals to Dionysus or Bacchus, the Greek and Roman gods of the grape and wine. Dionysus is often depicted covered in grape leaves. Wine is a symbol of blood, sacrifice, and youth, and Dionysus represents all of these things, as well as transformation and ecstasy. Festivals to Dionysus, called "Dionysia," often included frenzied dancing and drinking, and Dionysus was known as a god of fertility and fecundity. In some myths, his female followers, the maenads, were said to leave regular society and live wild in the woods, where they tore to pieces any man who dared set foot in their vicinity. At the Fall Equinox, some Wiccans make wine to honor Dionysus, and others just drink the wine and enjoy a little raucous Dionysia of their own.

As I already mentioned, the sabbat opposite the Fall Equinox on the wheel is the Spring Equinox. At the Spring

Equinox, the God, like the sun, is rising in his power, and at the Fall Equinox he is weakening or dying. Like on the Spring Equinox, Wiccans stop at the Fall Equinox and mark the day of balance, knowing that it is fleeting and powerful.

Decorations for a seasonal Fall Equinox altar might include pomegranates, grapes and grapevines, fall leaves, antlers, and cornstalks.

October 31: Samhain, Halloween

Most Wiccans refer to Halloween as Samhain, pronounced "sow-en." There was a crazy idea proposed by a nineteenth-century folklorist and picked up by several authors since that Samhain (or Sam Hain) is actually the name of the Celtic god of the dead, and some fundamentalist Christians (particularly the makers of Christian comic tracts who equate "god of the dead" with "Satan") perpetuate this argument. However, the word Samhain is really Irish for "November"—nothing fancy or occult about it at all.

Many Wiccans will tell you that Samhain is their favorite holiday, if only because they can walk among "normal" people without sticking out quite as much as they do the rest of the year. On Samhain, Wiccans believe that the otherworld is close at hand, so the beloved dead (and the not-so-beloved ones too) can cross over to visit the living. Some Wiccans think of Samhain as the Wiccan New Year, and some think of it as the third and final harvest.

In older days, Samhain was the time in the Northern Hemisphere when weaker animals were culled from a herd and killed, both to feed people during the winter and also so that feed could be conserved and used for the strongest animals. This is one of the reasons this holiday has such an association with blood and death. Blood, of course, represents the line of ancestry, and Wiccans welcome the return of their dead on Samhain. Many Wiccans create ancestor altars and rituals to encourage the spirits of their loved ones to return. Some prepare plates of food to leave out for the dead, and others conduct "dumb suppers," which are meals held entirely in silence, with a chair and plate of food set at the table for the dead.

This is another one of those nights when the fey are said to change residence. Many Samhain stories about the fey center around the wild hunt. The wild hunt is a procession of fairies through the sky, accompanied by the dead, those humans stuck in the land of the fey, and other spectral beings, all riding on animals. Some Wiccans believe that the fey are simply witches on "the other side." The wild hunt is led by the God in some stories, and sometimes by the Goddess. As I mentioned before, one of the aspects of the Wiccan God is the lord of the dead, so it seems fitting that he would lead the hunt.

As the lord of the dead, the God resides in the underworld, waiting to receive the souls of the dead and ready them for rebirth. The Goddess is bereft of the God at this time, but she is also pregnant with the future God. Some

Wiccans believe that the Goddess is in her crone or wise-woman phase at Samhain. The energy of this sabbat is turned inward, and during this time Wiccans enter a more reflective part of the year where they rest and wait for the rebirth of the God at Yule and later the spark of life at Imbolc.

Since, as Wiccans are fond of saying, on Samhain "the veil between the worlds is thin," it is a great time for divination. Although the association with Halloween and divination has been around for centuries, it grew considerably during the Victorian era, when young women in particular would use various crazy methods to try to determine whom they would marry. They would peel an apple all in one piece, throw the peel over their shoulder, and look for their love's initial to be spelled out in it, or roast chestnuts over a fire, giving each the name of a potential suitor and seeing which one popped first. Most Wiccans don't do these things, but they do whip out the tarot cards or the astrology charts around Samhain. If it is the Wiccan New Year, it's a good time to look ahead.

Most Wiccans embrace the secular trappings of Halloween as much as everyone else; the costumes, the parties, the pumpkins, the sweets, and the love of a good scare. Some Wiccans are offended by the image of the green-faced, pointy-hatted witch that flies by on her broom this time of year, but others celebrate her as a symbol of the survival of pagan tradition and feminine power. The green face represents, among other things, fertility (not sea sickness), as does the broom, and some see the pointy hat as a symbol of power.

Samhain and its opposite sabbat, Beltane, form the polarity of sex and death—the beginning and end of life. At Beltane in the British Isles, people would drive their cattle between two bonfires to enhance their fertility; at Samhain some of those cattle were slaughtered for the winter. At Beltane, the God and Goddess unite; at Samhain they are separated by death. Samhain has a serious, solemn element to it, but it is also a joyful time of games, memories, and reunion with those who have gone before.

Decorations for a seasonal Samhain altar might include pumpkins, divination tools such as a scrying mirror or tarot cards, apples, fall leaves, or skeletons.

December 21: Winter Solstice, Yule

The two most popular Christian holidays—Easter and Christmas—are also the two most pagan. Many Wiccans celebrate the Winter Solstice, more commonly called Yule, as the birth of the God, just as Christians do. At Yule, the new God comes to earth, bringing hope and light. Yule in the Northern Hemisphere is the shortest, darkest day of the year, but it is also the day when the shift toward the light and warmth begins. Some Wiccans believe that at Yule the Oak King, God of the light half of the year, defeats the Holly King, God of the dark half, who began his rule at the Summer Solstice.

Wiccans celebrate Yule by bringing holly or evergreen boughs into the house to encourage the growth of life and return of warmth. This may include a Christmas tree—a Yule tree, actually—decorated with symbols of the sun, among other things. There may also be wreaths and mistletoe. The mistletoe plant is a parasite of the oak tree, which may be another clue to the origin of the myth of the Oak King.

Like Imbolc, Wiccan Yule celebrations include a lot of candles and focus on fire and light. Wiccans with the luxury of a fireplace might burn a Yule log, lit with a piece of the log from the year before.

Wiccans tend to feast, give gifts, and focus on children at Yule, just as Christians do. Storytelling, games, and songs are common at Wiccan Yule rituals. Anything that brings joy into the darkest part of the year is welcome. The Goddess is sometimes honored as the mother of the God at Yule.

At the opposite sabbat, the Summer Solstice, the God reaches his peak, whereas at Yule he is just beginning his ascent. Where the Summer Solstice signals the beginning of a retraction—a going inward—Yule signals an outward flow of energy—an expansion.

Decorations for a seasonal Yule altar might include holly, mistletoe, pine cones, candles, and sun symbols.

As you learn more about Wicca, you will want to experiment with writing sabbat rituals and discover what symbols mean the most to you at each holiday. Supplement this brief introduction with material from books on the recommended reading list, practices you glean from other Wiccans, and your own personal experience. The next chapter will show you how to take all of the ritual components we've discussed and put them together into a complete ritual.

10

Putting It Together:

Using What You've Learned

So far, you've read some Wiccan theory; practiced feeling energy, grounding, and shielding; tried meditation and pathworking; and learned about the Wiccan circle, quarters and elements, gods, and sabbats. I'm assuming that if you waded through all that stuff, you're interested enough to try your first full Wiccan ritual, so in this chapter I'm going to show you how to tie everything you've learned together and create a Wiccan ritual that is meaningful for you. It's good to start with a sabbat, full moon, or special occasion that really speaks to you through image, symbol, or metaphor or just intrigues you, because your extra interest and curiosity will make the pieces of the ritual come together easily. I'm going to use a Samhain sabbat celebration as an example because lots of Wiccans love Samhain and the symbolism is easy to grasp, but feel free to create a ritual for whichever occasion you like.

Writing and Assembling Items for Your Ritual

Since this is your first sabbat, it's a good idea to start by doing some research. Yes, research can be a drag, but if you're interested in Wicca and the holiday you've chosen, it shouldn't be so bad, and often something you find in research will inspire you. Remember, one of the biggest pluses and minuses of Wicca is that there is no centralized priesthood, no one to tell you exactly what the sabbats and rituals should mean to you, so the burden and the privilege of figuring it out are yours alone. Look at the sabbat section of other Wicca books or on Wiccan Web sites. Look up the herbs and oils appropriate for Samhain in books or online. Post questions on a Wicca email list. Find out about the gods and goddesses (if any) associated with the sabbat. Check out some books on autumn folklore and customs. Meditate on what the holiday means to you, and ask others what it means to them. A note of caution: Just because something is written in a book, posted on the Internet, or stated in a Wicca email list or chat room doesn't mean it's true! Double-check your facts. There is a lot of great stuff online, but when it comes to Wicca, there is just as much garbage. I've listed some reasonably reliable books and resources at the end of this book.

Once you've done this, try to synthesize the information and distill it down to two or three pervasive themes that appeal to you. For the purposes of the example, let's say that you've done some research on Samhain, and you want to focus on it as the entry into the darkest part of the year and include some kind of ritual in honor of your ancestors. With that in mind, you will need to decide exactly how you'd like to honor the ancestors. In our training circles, we often light candles for them, include their photographs on the altar, and prepare a special plate of food for them. You may want to write something to say to each of the ancestors with whom you had a special relationship or something that you can say to all of them collectively. If someone you love passed away in the last year, be sure to include a special statement for him or her. Don't forget animals, either. It's our experience that when we call our beloved dead on Samhain, the spirits of our pets show up alongside those of our families.

Once you have a plan for the central part of your ritual, it's time to collect the things you'll need to carry it out. For this Samhain ritual, you might find:

- A black or white candle for each ancestor you want to call out specifically or one candle for all of them.
- A cauldron with kitty litter or a candle holder for the ancestor candle(s).
- A special plate of your ancestors' favorite foods (don't romanticize here—if they loved Twinkies and pork rinds, include Twinkies and pork rinds).

- An extra cup or chalice for the ancestors.
- A carved jack-o'-lantern with a candle inside (to use as a lantern to light their way).
- Photographs of your ancestors (if the photos are not framed, consider putting them in a frame or protecting them in a plastic bag because they tend to end up damaged by dripping candle wax, wine, or saltwater).

- A bottle of wine or juice and a corkscrew.
- A plate with three small cakes (cookies work well) for the cakes and wine ceremony (which I will explain in the next section).
- A small bowl to make a libation (also explained in the next section).
- A small amount of oil to anoint the ancestor candle (this can be a scented oil that you associate with Samhain or your ancestors, or just plain olive oil—if you use an essential oil blend, do your homework and make sure that it's okay to get it on your skin).
- A CD player and music that inspires you (optional).
- Samhain-style altar decorations.
- Your ritual tools, including the broom, bowls of salt and water, a candle and holder each for the Goddess and the God (and statues if you have them), your athame, a candle and holder for each quarter, incense and burner (you can find special Samhain incense in

many occult shops or online), and your chalice or a wineglass.

- Matches or a lighter.

You may not need all of these things when you are writing your own ritual, but I wanted to include them here so you can see how they are used.

Some Bells and Whistles

There are three small pieces that are common in Wiccan rituals that I haven't introduced to you yet: the circle blessing, the cakes and wine ceremony, and libations. As with everything in Wiccan practice, not all Wiccans use these components. I am going to include them in the Samhain ritual so you can see them in context.

Circle Blessing

Many Wiccans like to make a circle blessing after the circle is drawn and the quarters and God and Goddess are called. The blessing serves as a statement that the circle is complete, it is sacred space, and the stage is set for whatever ritual you are going to do. It fixes the circle between the worlds. The blessing and certain other parts of a Wiccan ritual often end with the phrase "So mote it be." Essentially, this is Wiccan for "It is this way because I say so and it is my will." Here is a sample circle blessing:

> *Great God and Goddess, I have built this circle with love and honor. It is a holy place between the human world and the spirit realm, where I work my will in both. So mote it be.*

Cakes and Wine Ceremony

In the cakes and wine ceremony, Wiccans bless a chalice of wine and a plate of cakes in honor of the God and Goddess. The wine and cup symbolize the blood and womb of the Goddess, and the cakes are made from grain, a symbol of the God. They are consumed together in acknowledgment of the union of the God and Goddess and its result—the fruits of the earth that sustain human life. In a simple cakes and wine ceremony, Wiccans will put the plate of cakes and cup of wine on the altar, hold the athame over them, and visualize the energy of the God and Goddess infusing them while saying something simple like:

> *I bless these cakes and wine in the names of the Great God and Goddess.*

Libations

Some Wiccans, our group included, like to make libations to the God and Goddess within the circle. What this means is that we set aside some of whatever we eat or drink in circle to be given back to the gods. We put the libations in a bowl or on a plate and set it in the garden. When Wiccans do a cakes and wine ceremony, they will often consecrate one extra cake and place it in the libation bowl along with some of the wine from the cup. If Wiccans share a meal or treat in circle (we sometimes jokingly call these "snackraments"), they will put a little bit of each food or beverage in the bowl too.

You may wish to consider writing or finding your own versions of each of these extra pieces.

Personal Preparation

There are two additional things that Wiccans often do before ritual: They take a ritual bath or shower and decide what to wear.

Ritual Bath

It's considered bad form to enter a Wiccan circle without having had a bath or shower. It's disrespectful to the gods, and, depending on how long it's been since you had your last bath or shower, it's distracting for anyone else who may be circling with you. Many Wiccans see a ritual bath as a chance to slough off whatever unwanted energy or mood they picked up during the day and prepare to enter sacred space. It can help set the mood and intent for your ritual too.

A ritual bath doesn't have to be anything fancy. It can be just a regular bath or shower. I know one Wiccan who puts some salt and warm water in a cup and dumps it over his head while he's showering, and you can simply add some salt to your bathwater, if you'd like. You can bathe with special soap, bath salts, or oils that are associated with the sabbat or magic you will be doing in your circle too. Again, remember to read up on oils and herbs before putting them in the bath. Some will burn your skin, and others are toxic. Oils tend to float on the surface in little bubbles, so don't count on the water to dilute them.

You can also burn incense and candles and listen to music in the bathroom to set the mood. Be careful to put the candles in safe places and keep the CD player away from the tub.

Ritual Wear

Someone could write an entire book on Wiccan ritual garb, or the lack thereof. Wiccans frequently make or buy special robes to wear in ritual. They may have one robe that they wear all the time, or have robes in several colors so they can switch with the seasons. If you're not great with a sewing machine and you don't know anyone who is, you can find robes online or in some occult shops. Often there are ads in the back of Wiccan magazines or on Web sites for people who will sew custom ritual robes. If you can't find a good robe, check out used-clothing stores for kimonos. They make great robes. In a pinch, a silky bathrobe will do, if you can find one that doesn't look too much like lingerie.

Some Wiccans have special clothes that they wear only in ritual. These can be anything that makes the Wiccan feel like he or she is dressed to enter sacred space: dresses, skirts, tunics, loose pants, kilts, hats—you name it. If they practice outside, Wiccans may wear cloaks. Somehow, down jackets and polar fleece don't seem very special, but I've seen those in outdoor ritual circles too. Many Wiccans go barefoot in circle, but this is not required, and some Wiccans have special ritual shoes or boots. Socks are a good idea if you live in a cool climate or have cold floors.

Some Wiccans circle naked, which they refer to with the rather fanciful phrase "going skyclad," or clothed only by the sky. The idea is that there is no robe or clothing more sacred than the skin you were born in. Some Wiccans think it's easier to raise energy if you're naked because the energy is not blocked by clothing, but I've never found this to be true. If you're circling alone or with a group of people you trust, you may want to try going skyclad. It's very liberating, and once you're partway into the ritual, you tend to forget you're naked—unless you bump into a candle or spill wine on yourself, that is. If you're planning a skyclad circle and you live in a cold climate, turn up the heat for a while beforehand or put a space heater in the room for a few minutes. Otherwise you may gain a new understanding of that old cliché "cold as a witch's . . ." (you know what I mean).

Many Wiccans love ritual jewelry. They may wear it all the time or save it for circle, but you do not have to wear jewelry to be a Wiccan. Many Wiccans will consecrate their primary pieces of ritual jewelry, just as you consecrated your tools in chapter 8, because they see the jewelry as a spiritual tool and wearing it as a way to align with deity. Certain Wiccan traditions have special jewelry that is worn by people of different rank, necklaces made out of certain tradition-specific materials, or rings and bracelets engraved with special symbols. Others allow no jewelry in circle, or no jewelry made of certain materials or manmade ones. Still others have no rules about jewelry at all, although it's considered bad form if you're wearing enough that if you fell into a river wearing it, it would weigh you down and you'd drown. Don't laugh; go to any open public Wiccan ritual and you'll see at least one person yoked with the Wiccan equivalent of the British crown jewels.

When people become Wiccan, they will often purchase silver pentacles as a symbol of their path. Sometimes new Wiccans receive these as gifts at their initiations or dedications. A Wiccan pentacle necklace can be simple or ornate, but remember that there is a long-standing joke that you can always tell a new Wiccan because he or she will be the one wearing a pentacle the size of a hood ornament. If you live in an area that is not Wicca-friendly, or if you fear that "outing" yourself could result in the loss of your job, you may wish to wear your pentacle under your clothes, save it for circle, forego it entirely, or choose a different Wiccan-friendly symbol that is not as recognizable by non-Wiccans, such as an ankh, a moon, or an animal that is associated with your favorite god or goddess. Some people forego the pentacle because it doesn't "speak" to them. You don't have to wear one to be Wiccan. I have plenty of magical jewelry, but I don't think I've worn a pentacle for fifteen years.

There is a staggering selection of Wiccan jewelry for sale. Some is commercially produced, and other pieces are handmade by Wiccan craftspeople. Some Wiccans prefer the handmade kind because they want to support Wiccan jewelry makers. Some believe that a handmade piece feels more personal and they can make it their own more readily than if it was mass-produced. Others just buy what's pretty or significant to them or make their own.

Performing the Ritual

Now that you've decided what you want to do, written the pieces you needed to write, assembled your ritual items, and figured out how you'd like to dress, it's time to put all of the components you've learned together. The following is a step-by-step walk-through of our example Samhain ritual. I've written it to be performed by one person alone. You can use this ritual as is, but better yet, use it as a springboard to write your own ritual.

1. Assemble your ritual items and set up your altar in the center of your circle space. Do not light any of the candles yet, but get everything ready. Remove the incense or charcoal from the package and put it in the censer, and place the bottle of wine, corkscrew, plate of ancestor food, extra cup, and plate of cakes under the altar if possible, or in front of it on the floor. Make sure your matches or lighter and the special oil you chose are within easy reach. Place an unlit candle in a holder of some kind in each quarter. If you are going to use a cauldron in the ritual, place it in the west, the direction of the ancestors and the dead (some use the north instead). If you're using the candle holder instead for the ancestor candle(s), put it on the altar. Set the carved jack-o'-lantern in the west. Set the pictures of your ancestors either on the altar or in the west with the pumpkin and cauldron. Shut the door to the circle room if you have pets.

2. Take your ritual bath, and dress in the clothes you have chosen for the rite. Ground.

3. Cleanse the ritual space as you did in chapter 5 (see the section "Preparing the Space"). Using the broom is particularly appropriate for Samhain. (You can ride it if you want—nobody is looking.)

4. Using your athame, draw your circle, starting in the north. I chose the north because many associate it with the Goddess and earth, and since Samhain is a holiday about death and rebirth, it seems appropriate that you begin and end your circle in the direction of the earth that gives us life and receives us in death. (Start in a different direction, if you'd like.)

5. Using the tip of your athame, drop three scoops of salt in the bowl of water, then stir. Wipe off the blade. If you don't want your blade in saltwater, pick up the salt, drop it in the water, and stir with your fingers. Take the bowl of saltwater, and starting in the north, move around your circle, sprinkling the saltwater along the edge of the circle.

6. Return to the altar and light the charcoal or incense stick. Put loose incense on the charcoal, and, beginning in the north, carefully walk around your circle with the smoking censer. If your censer is too hot to pick up, you can either bring an oven mitt into the circle or fan the incense smoke in each direction.

7. Take your athame and go to the north once more. Invoke the power of the north by lighting the north candle, drawing the pentagram, and saying something like:

Spirits of the north, power of earth, I call you to join my circle.

8. Repeat in the other three quarters, changing east to "power of air," south to "power of fire," and west to "power of water."

9. Light the God candle, stand with your arms raised in a Y position, and invoke the God, saying something like:

   I light this candle for the God.
   Lord of the sun and grain,
   Lord of the hunt and underworld,
   Lord of death and rebirth,
   Be here this night in my sacred Samhain circle.

10. Light the Goddess candle, stand with your arms raised in a Y position, and invoke the Goddess, saying something like:

    I light this candle for the Goddess.
    Lady of the heavens and earth,
    Lady of the moon and the mysteries,
    Mother of us all,
    Be here this night in my sacred Samhain circle.

11. Do your circle blessing:

    Great God and Goddess, I have built this circle with love. It is a holy place between the human world and the spirit realm, where I honor you and work my will. So mote it be.

12. Light the candle in the jack-o'-lantern, and say something like:

    Friends, loved ones, and Wiccans past, it is Samhain, and the veil between the worlds is thin. Join me and celebrate.

13. Return to the altar, take your ancestor candle, and anoint it with a little bit of the oil. As you rub the oil into the candle, speak to the ancestor(s) the candle represents. Tell him or her anything you would if he or she were standing in front of you. Don't be afraid to laugh or cry if you are moved to. If you have nothing profound to say, simply welcome him or her. When you have anointed the candle and finished speaking, light it and place it either in the cauldron of rebirth or in the holder on the altar. If you are using multiple candles to represent several different ancestors, repeat this process with each candle until you are finished.

14. Take the plate of ancestor food and hold it over the altar, saying something like:

    I dedicate this meal to my friends and loved ones who have passed beyond the veil and returned to me this night. I am always with you, as you are with me. Blessed be.

15. Place the ancestor plate and extra cup (empty) in the west.

16. Sit in front of the altar, relax, and allow yourself to meditate or commune with the spirits of your loved ones. Think about how they affected your life and the good times you had together. If you weren't moved to speak when you anointed the candles, you may wish to address your ancestors now.

17. When you are finished, open the wine if you haven't already, and pour some in your chalice. Place the plate of cakes on the altar. Bless the cakes and wine by holding your hands over them, drawing energy up from the earth, and visualizing the energy infusing the cakes and wine, while saying something like:

    I bless these cakes and wine in the names of the Great God and Goddess.

18. Raise the cup of wine over the altar to salute the God and Goddess and raise it to the west to salute the ancestors. Pour a little wine from your chalice into the libation bowl, then pour some in the empty ancestor cup. Drink the rest of the wine in your cup.

19. Salute the God and Goddess and the ancestors with the plate of cakes. Drop one cake in the libation bowl, put one on the ancestor plate, and eat the third yourself.

20. When you are finished, thank your ancestors for joining you by facing west and saying something like:

Friends and loved ones, thank you for your presence here tonight. Your visit has filled me with joy. Return now to the world of spirit. So mote it be.

21. Blow out the candle in the pumpkin. You can leave the ancestor candles burning or blow them out now too.

22. Face the altar, raise your arms in the Y position, and thank the God and Goddess for joining you by saying something like:

    Great God and Goddess, thank you for joining me and blessing my Samhain rite. Hail, and farewell.

23. Extinguish the God and Goddess candles.

24. Go to the north and release the north quarter by drawing the banishing pentagram and saying something like:

    Spirits of the north, thank you for attending my rite. Farewell.

25. Extinguish the north candle, and repeat with the other three quarters, going around counterclockwise.

26. Return to the north, and take up the circle using your athame, moving around the edge counterclockwise. Remember to ground out the energy. Do not keep it in your body.

27. Ground again to make sure you have pushed all the excess earth energy out of your body.
28. If you left the ancestor candles burning, keep an eye on them until they go out, or put them out now.
29. Take the libation bowl and ancestor plate outside. We usually put the contents of the libation bowl in the compost and the ancestor plate in the garden. We return for the empty plate a day or two later.

You've just completed a full Wiccan sabbat ritual. Write about your experiences in your journal or book of shadows. Make note of what worked and what didn't, and what messages, if any, you got from your loved ones. Tracking these things will help you discover what really speaks to you in ritual.

11

So You're Curious about Magic . . .

MANY PEOPLE ARE DRAWN initially to Wicca because Wiccans do magic. They may have been sucked in by the coolness factor, but in many cases, beneath the desire for the glitz and glamour they also seem to harbor a deep need for personal transformation and taking control of their lives. This is a good thing, because there's really no glamour in magic, despite what prime-time television shows would have you believe. Magic is challenging, empowering, and rewarding work. Magic is working your will.

What Is Magic?

As I mentioned in chapter 2, one of the most commonly used definitions of magic among Wiccans is Aleister Crowley's definition, or some variation of it: Magic is "the science and art of causing change to occur in conformance with will." The first part of that definition is something most of us can relate to—no matter how great our lives are, there are always things that we would like to change. Wiccans do "everyday" magic to bring about things that they want—a new job, love, healing—and if you have read anything at all about Crowley you know that he was not a man to deny himself his wants either. But Crowley is not talking simply about working magic to bring about what you want, he is talking also about working your will. In addition to its mundane uses, magic has a "higher" purpose—to bring us closer to the divine; to align us with the patterns of nature and the universe that we must understand in order for our magic to work. When you perform a magical act in accordance with your true will, you are in harmony with deity. Working magic brings about change in the world, but it also brings about transformation in us. That said, magic does not have to be complex. Some of the simplest magics are the most effective. But it is important to remember that working magic is more than fulfilling everyday needs and wishes.

What Is a Spell?

When Wiccans explain what a spell is to non-Wiccans, they will sometimes say, "A spell is like a prayer." I disagree. Although in both a prayer and a spell you are making your desires known to the universe, the similarities end there. When you pray for something, you are asking God to help you achieve some goal. When you do a spell, you are telling the universe that you intend to bring about a certain change and you are putting the energy in motion to achieve that end. You may ask for help from a god or goddess in your spell, but it is really you who is doing the work and moving the energy behind your desired change.

A spell is a set of actions done in a specific sequence to manifest your intent. In less lofty terms, it is a recipe to bring about change, but instead of sugar, flour, and eggs, the ingredients are things like candles, oils, and herbs, and instead of sifting, stirring, or baking, the instructions may include visualization, gestures, chants or singing, dance or movement, meditation, invocation, and concentration. A basic spell format is to create ritual space, state your intent, visualize your goal, raise energy, send the energy to your goal, ground the extra energy, and close the ritual. When you do a spell, you are working with the power and energy patterns of nature. It's not supernatural, and it's not rocket science.

Spells usually have a spoken component where the person performing the magic states his or her intent. Often this is done in rhyme, because for many people it's easier to memorize rhyme, and if you're working with a group, the rhyming words and meter make it easier for the entire group to say the words together. Rhymes are also helpful because you can chant them over and over again to raise energy. As with the quarter calls and invocations, however, your spells do not have to rhyme to work, and if you think that your rhymes would either trip you up or make you laugh uncontrollably in the middle of your spell, or if your attempts at meter sound like a car with only three tires going over a pothole, it's best to skip the fancy stuff and just say what your intent is clearly and concisely without rhyme. The point, after all, is to work your will, not ace your poetry final.

In spell work, Wiccans also raise energy to direct toward the goal of the spell. There are endless techniques to raise energy, some of which are listed in chapter 3. A few of the most common are clapping, dancing, or singing, usually starting slowly and building in speed and intensity to a crescendo. When the energy is rising, many Wiccans will visualize it taking the form of a cone, which they call the "cone of power." The cone is usually centered over the altar, if you're using one, or centered in the circle. When the cone has reached its peak, the Wiccan(s) doing the spell releases it, sending the energy forth to put his or her intent in motion.

Correspondences

In order to work magic effectively, it's important to understand a little bit about magical correspondences. Correspondences are things that "go with" other things. They have similar qualities or similar energy. There is a basic magical concept that we touched on briefly in the ethics section in chapter 2: Like attracts like. The idea is that things that are similar are bound together energetically, and including one in a spell might attract the other; for example, using green candles (the color of American money) in a money spell, or heart-shaped items in a love spell.

When I was a kid, there was a clothing line for children called "Garanimals." Each item had a tag on it shaped like an animal. If you were fashion-impaired like I was, and you wanted a shirt to match a skirt you had picked out, you'd go look for shirts with the same animal on the tag as the skirt. If your skirt had a lion tag, you'd choose a shirt with a lion tag to match—a brilliant marketing idea that probably saved countless nerdy kids like me from certain fashion disaster. Unfortunately, there is no Garanimals guide to magical correspondences. There is no one book that will tell you everything you need to know. There are, however, many, many partial lists of correspondences in basic Wicca books and basic astrology books. I've included some of these books in the suggested reading list.

Other people's lists are a good place to start exploring correspondences, but remember that sometimes correspondences are subjective, especially color correspondences. For example, you might associate red with health because it is the color of blood and vitality, but someone else might associate white with health because of its link to cleanliness and purity. Who is right? The answer is that, to some extent anyway, whoever is doing the magic is right. If white is the color that works for you, that seems to align with your purpose and helps you visualize your goal, then white is right, no matter what anyone else says. Herb and astrological correspondences tend to be less subjective (although sometimes there is quibbling about what goes with what there too), and

I've included some sources for those in the reading list as well.

Twelve Steps for a Great Spell

In basic Wicca books you can find any number of spells already written and ready to use. I encourage you to try some of the pre-written ones, but I encourage you even more to write your own spells. Your spells are more potent than anything anyone else could write for you because they are composed of pieces that are significant to you personally. In addition, writing your own spells is a powerful statement that you are not just doing everyday magic; you are also working your will on that higher magical level. So, if you're ready to take this piece of your spiritual growth in your own hands, here are twelve steps to building a great spell.

Step 1: Set your goal.

What is the goal of your spell? Write it down. Be specific! There's a great scene in the film *The Joy Luck Club* where a Chinese girl who knows that she will not be able to choose her own husband prays that he will not be old and ugly. After her wedding, when her veil is removed and she sees her new husband for the first time, she discovers that he's not old or ugly, but he has barely hit puberty and he's childish and immature. She got her wish, but not in the way she thought she might because she wasn't specific in her wish. I was in a sweat lodge once, and a man in the lodge asked Creator for strength. As if they had planned it beforehand, everyone in the lodge moved away from him simultaneously. They did this because they knew that the best way to become strong is to face adversity, and they didn't want to share in the little "life lesson" he had just set himself up for. If you ask for something in the presence of the Creator or the gods and aren't specific, chances are the powers-that-be are going to see to it that you reach your magical goal the hard way. It's not malicious; it's just the way life works.

If you're doing magic to bring love into your life, what kind of love are you looking for? Romantic? Friendship? Brotherly love? What kind of person would you like to attract? Don't think of or name a specific person, because you don't want to manipulate someone into a relationship with you, but do think of traits you'd like him or her to have, including whether you'd rather it was a him or a her. Remember too that even though you are a super-powerful Wiccan-in-the making, don't set a vague and huge magical goal like "world peace." Noble as this sounds, it's too big a topic with too many variables for one lone Wiccan to achieve. I'm not telling you to aim lower than whatever height you're capable of (that wouldn't be working your will, after all), but when you're starting out, it's best to choose smaller, more concrete objectives.

Step 2: Examine your will.

Is the magic you are contemplating aligned with your higher purpose? If you don't know, don't do the magic until you have meditated on this question or asked deity or your inner self for guidance. You may also want to use divination, like tarot cards or astrology, to help you determine if this spell is right for you.

Step 3: Consider your ethics and the possible consequences.

Think about possible outcomes of your actions and their impact before proceeding. Will what you are contemplating hurt you or others? Remember the Wiccan Rede and the Threefold Law, and act for the highest good. But it's also important not to kneecap yourself in trying to avoid harm by creating a wimpy spell. A wimpy spell won't help you and may impede your true will rather than help you align with it. This is another area where divination can help you make a decision.

Step 4: Work toward your goal on the mundane plane.

Magic is much more effective if in addition to doing a spell you also try to achieve your goal the "everyday" way. After all, you can't win the lottery if you don't buy a ticket, and it's hard to get a new job if you don't send out any resumes, no matter how kick-ass your spell is.

Step 5: Choose the best time to perform your magic.

When is the most appropriate time to do the working? There are lots of factors to consider in choosing the right time. The first is simply: When do you have time to do it? You don't want to be rushed. You also want to choose a time when you are rested and alert. As with examining your will and possible consequences, you might want to do divination to determine the best time to work your spell.

Another factor, and one that's easy to determine, is the phase of the moon. Wiccans do magic to enhance things or draw things to them—such as health, money, and love magic—while the moon is waxing, or getting bigger in the sky. They do magic to banish things or make things smaller—such as magic to reduce debt, lose weight, or break bad habits—when the moon is waning, or getting smaller in the sky. Magic to bring things to fruition is often done at the full moon. So how do you tell if the moon is waxing or waning? The easiest way is to look up at the sky. The moon is waxing when the light side is curved to the right, like a capital *D*. It's waning when the light side is curved to the left, like a capital *C*. If it's too cloudy to tell, it's easy to find the phase of the moon by searching on the Internet or consulting an astrological calendar.

You can also plan spell work based on the day of the week. Each day is associated with a planet, and the planets in turn have their own correspondences. Sunday is associated with the Sun, and is good for magic that has to do with energy and the life force, money, and prosperity in general. Monday is associated with the Moon, and is a good time to do magic for conception and anything having to do with mothers, emotional work, and nurture. Tuesday is associated with Mars, the warrior planet, and is good for any kind of protective or aggressive magic, and especially for magic to muster up the guts to stand up for yourself. Wednesday is associated with the planet Mercury, named after the Roman messenger of the gods, so magic having to do with communication and travel works well on this day. Thursday is associated with the planet Jupiter, Roman king of the gods, and magic for things like money, luck, and fortune is enhanced. Friday is associated with Venus, planet of love, so magic to draw love, send love, or heal relationships works well on Friday, provided all involved parties consent to the working. Saturday is associated with Saturn, the planet of work, boundaries, and restrictions, so protection magic, magic to eliminate debt, or magic to find employment work well on Saturday. This list of associations with the days of the week is not exhaustive.

There is a lot more to magical timing, but the previous factors are a good start. Entire books have been written on magical timing, and I've included some good ones in the recommended reading list.

Step 6: Involve other people (or not).

Who will be involved in your ritual? If you are planning to do it alone, this is an easy question to answer. However, you may wish to include others. Who is likely to share your goal and be willing and able to help you? If you are planning to do magic that involves another person who won't be present—like doing healing work for your grandmother, for example—you should contact the person if possible and ask his or her permission before proceeding. Sometimes it is impossible to get permission, like if your grandmother is on a respirator or unconscious. In those cases, meditate on whether the spell is appropriate, and use your knowledge of your grandmother to help you decide.

Step 7: Involve otherwordly beings (or not).

As I said earlier, magic is different than praying because you are the primary force behind making it work. However, you may wish to ask for help from the God and Goddess, your personal deities, animal "familiars," ancestors, or elemental beings. Before you begin, do some research to determine whom it would be most appropriate to ask. As long as the magic is positive, the God and Goddess are good choices for just about anything, but the God is particularly helpful in work that has to do with protection, fertility, nature, death, raw energy, and animals, and the Goddess is particularly helpful in magic about birth, fertility, plants, the earth, and manifesting things into your life. Your personal deities will have characteristics associated with them that could help you too. For example, the Celtic goddess Cerridwen is linked to wisdom, and the Greek god Hermes is related to travel.

There are two types of Wiccan animal familiars: discarnate (spirits in animal form) and incarnate (living pets or other animals). Discarnate animal familiars or spirits serve as guides and helpers. Many Wiccans work with animal spirits, but some do not. In the accounts of the witch trials, there are stories of animal familiars, most of which were said to be demons in animal form. Wiccan familiars are not demons. They are positive energy spirits or thoughtforms that take animal shapes in the mind of the Wiccan. Some Wiccans choose the familiar they would like to work with based on its qualities. For example, they might choose a raven for its intelligence or a wolf for its strength. Sometimes an animal familiar chooses the Wiccan. I have a student who seems to have been chosen by rats and another by spiders—not animals either would have gravitated toward naturally. Some Wiccans work with their pets and believe them to be familiar spirits incarnate. I have a cat that loves to "help" with my husband's massage clients. She lies down next to them, stretches out a paw to touch them, and does some weird energy thing that nobody quite understands, but several of his return customers specifically request that she be allowed in the room to do whatever it is she does. Many pets are drawn to energy. If you have a pet that really seems to want to join you in circle, consider letting him or her in, as long as it's safe (no open flame, no incense if your pet is a bird or reptile because they have delicate lungs, no poisonous oils or plants to ingest by accident, and so on). Watch them around your plate of cakes. My cats have been known to run off with ritual food.

You can always call on your ancestors to help in magic. They are linked to you both in blood and spirit, and they can be powerful allies. Some ancestors will not come when you call, and some will not approve of you doing spells, especially if they followed a different religion when they were alive. Never ask an ancestor whom you think might be offended. If you think they're okay with magic, however, call on them to strengthen your work.

Last but not least, you can call on the spirits of the elements. If you are doing a spell that involves bravery, for example, you might call fire spirits (keep that fire extinguisher handy), or if you are doing one that requires intellect, you might call on air spirits.

Step 8: Choose the location.

There are many places where you could do your spell: inside versus outside being the first consideration, followed by whether or not you will be able to work without interruption. You will want to choose a place that is easy to get to and where you have access to whatever you need for the spell. The nature of your spell will be a determining factor too. If you're working with fire or nature spirits, you might want to do it outside, but if you're doing a quiet working that requires a lot of concentration or meditation, it might be better to be inside. You'll also need to consider whether you want to do your spell in sacred space. Casting a circle is not at all required for magic, but it's a good idea if you are calling the gods.

Step 9: Choose your correspondences.

Magic works well when your spell includes items that are aligned with your goal. These items help focus your intent and add energy to the working. When you are thinking about what items to include in your spell, consider things whose color, sound, scent, taste, or texture somehow suits your goals. Consider food, candles, oils, incense, magical tools, clothing, herbs, and rocks and crystals that are associated with the purpose of your spell.

Step 10: Write or acquire the spell.

Do you want to write your own spell, or have you found one in a book? If you've found one, do you want to modify it to suit you better? Do you want to go into your spell with a carefully determined script, or do you want to have a general idea of what you'd like to do and make the words up on the fly?

If you choose to write your spell, first think of your goal. Find a way to state your goal clearly in words, either with rhyme or without. Then build the ritual around this center statement of intent. Incorporate the correspondences you've chosen, either directly into the words or into the greater ritual. The steps of the spell ritual can be very similar to the steps you've been using in the other rituals in this book. For example:

1. Clean and prepare your space. Set up the altar and draw a circle.
2. Call the quarters, if desired.
3. Call the God and Goddess, if desired.
4. Declare your intent, speak the words of your spell, and focus on your goal.
5. Raise energy to direct toward your goal using any one of many methods, including breath work, dance and other physical movement, chant, tai chi, or visualization. If you'd like, see the energy as a rising cone of power in the center of your space.
6. Focus and direct the energy. Visualize your goal, and mentally direct the energy to it.

7. Ground and release excess energy.
8. Thank all participating beings, human and otherwise.
9. Say farewell to the God and Goddess, release the quarters, take up the circle, and clear the space.
10. Reinforce the spell by repeating it later if necessary. Sometimes it takes more than one shot.

Remember, you do not have to build a circle, call the quarters, or call the gods. I have included those steps in case you want to do them. It might be best to use them during your first few tries.

Step 11: Prepare.

Sometimes Wiccans will do preparatory work that helps them begin to align with their purpose before they ever start the actual spell. This may include taking a ritual bath with herbs or oils associated with their goal (for example, basil for a money spell), fasting for a day, eating foods that are aligned with the goal, and charging/blessing/consecrating tools and materials prior to the ritual.

Step 12: Work your magic and **know** *that it will succeed.*

A Sample Spell

The following is an oldie but goodie: a spell for a witches' bottle. A witches' bottle is a charm to protect your home. It consists of a bottle or jar filled with sharp objects, such as pins and needles; pieces of string; and a liquid, often red wine. The bottle is filled during the ritual, sealed, and buried in the yard after the ritual is ended. The idea is that the sharp items drive away harm, the strings bind it up, and the liquid dilutes it or washes it away. When you make a witches' bottle, you do not do it with the intent to harm anyone, just to drive bad energy and burglars away. So what does a witches' bottle have to do with all that lofty, noble stuff I said earlier about working your will? Well, it's not the most sophisticated spell, but it gets to the core: If you don't have safe, stable space in which to live and practice your spirituality, you will have a hard time finding your higher purpose.

You can do this spell either inside or outside of a circle. It's a spell that's been around for a long time, it's true "kitchen witch" magic, and I suspect that whoever made it up years and years ago was thinking more about protecting his or her home and family than the intricacies of ritual. Since we've talked about ritual structure a lot already, I'm just going to include the central piece of the working; the guts of the spell. You can add the circle and other ritual elements if you feel they are appropriate.

You'll see when you get into the spell that I've broken the "statement of intent" into four pieces: one for the sharp things, one for the threads, one for the wine, and one for the whole bottle.

You will need:

- A glass bottle with a tight-fitting lid or cork. Empty spice jars work well.
- Sharp items such as pins, razor blades, nails, needles, and tacks in a bowl or other container (not in the bottle yet).
- Several short strings or threads, preferably black, but any color will do.
- Red wine or another liquid. Red corresponds to aggression and protection.
- A black candle. Red is okay too. Black corresponds to banishing, and red to strength.
- Matches or a lighter.

The Spell

1. Prepare your ritual space, if desired. Ground.
2. Open the circle, if desired.
3. Slowly begin dropping the sharp items in the jar. Be careful not to cut yourself. As you place each item in, visualize negative energy being repelled from your home. If you want, say something like:

   Pins and needles, razors and tacks,
   Drive all harmful energy back.

4. When the jar is about two-thirds full of the sharp things, place several strings and threads in the jar. Visualize negative energy being bound up in the threads as you do this. If you want, say something like:

    Pieces of thread, pieces of string,
    Bind up harmful, negative things.

5. Pour some wine into the jar to fill the spaces between the other items. Leave a small amount of space at the top. Visualize the wine washing away all negative stuff that might approach your home. If you want, say something like:

    Reddest wine, protect this place,
    Wash all harm out of my space.

6. Cap the jar tightly. Light the black candle, and drip candle wax all the way around the edge of the jar. As you do this, visualize and know that your spell is fixed and it will work.

7. Raise energy and send it into the bottle. You can do this by pulling earth energy up from your taproot and running it into the bottle through your hands. You can also repeat the following chant faster and faster until you feel the energy is peaking, and then direct the energy into the bottle.

    All harm banish,
    Be gone, vanish!

8. Push all the energy into the bottle. Do not keep any of it in your body. After the bottle is charged, ground.

9. Thank the gods and quarters, and take up the circle if you cast one.

10. Allow the wax on the bottle to cool and harden. Take the bottle outside and bury it in your front yard or in front of your building, preferably in a corner. Visualize it sending out an energetic barrier that repels harmful things. Know that it will protect you. Reinforce the magic from time to time by visualizing the bottle repelling harm from your home, perhaps at each full moon.

You've done your first spell!

12

Where Do I Go from Here?

Now you know a little bit about the beliefs, practices, deities, tools, and techniques of Wicca. If you want to learn more, what do you do next? The obvious answer is to read more about Wicca. There are some good Wicca books on the market (and some lousy ones too), and there is information in magazines such as *NewWitch* and on the Web. Read a variety of things from a variety of sources. Check out both scholarly and anecdotal material and the resource list in this book. Build a base of knowledge.

But remember, reading is not enough. Wicca is not a "religion of the book." It is about engaging with life, and it requires active participation and practice over time. So do the exercises in this and other basic Wicca books. Begin assembling your own Wiccan practice. Explore the Wiccan ideas that sing to you, and create some rituals for yourself. Build an altar. Talk to the gods. Start a book of shadows. Most of all, open yourself up to the transformation and self-discovery that walking the Wiccan path can inspire.

You've probably figured out by now that you can't snap your fingers or wiggle your nose and instantly become a Wiccan. It takes months, years, sometimes decades to hone all of the skills used in Wicca and to work the mysteries with any depth. Nothing ticks off established Wiccans—those who have actually done the work and walked the talk that goes along with the title of Wiccan—more than a "newbie" who reads a Wicca book and declares himself Lord High Priest Dragonsbane of the Moonbeam and Fairydust Tradition or some such pompous, ridiculous title. If you do this, the Wiccan community will give you another name: fluff bunny. Fluff bunnies are poseurs, people who have read a few books and lit a candle or two and therefore think they know everything about Wicca, or people who treat Wicca as though it were a live-action fantasy role-playing game—in other words, people who claim to follow the path but don't respect it. So read, but don't stop there. Wicca is about change and transformation after all, so stopping after you've got a book or two under your belt won't cut it.

What can you do in addition to studying and practicing by yourself? That will depend on you, your preferences, and the opportunities available to you. There are several questions that potential Wiccans ask once they have read about Wicca and decided that they want to learn more. If you are interested in continuing, it's important that you answer these questions for yourself and/or ask them of others. The answers will help you shape your next steps.

Should I Work Alone or in a Group?

There is no central church of Wicca (thank the Goddess). There is no authority that tells Wiccans how they must worship, when, and with whom. The upside of this is that Wiccans have the freedom to practice their religion in whatever way they see fit. The downside is that sometimes it's difficult to find support, camaraderie, or other people to practice with (if you want to). Most Wiccans practice their religion either in small, autonomous, family-like groups called covens; large public gatherings; "solitary," meaning alone; or some combination of these. Ultimately, all Wiccans are solitary at some point because their relationship with their deities is personal, and it exists whether they're working with a group or not. So if you do decide you'd like to work with a group, it's best if you also become a strong solitary Wiccan.

Advantages of Group Work

Some of the advantages of working in groups are that you have others with whom you can share the work and bounce ideas around. You have support and people who understand what you're trying to achieve (most of the time, anyway). Others can help you validate and interpret your experiences and keep you from feeling alone. Each member of a group has strengths and weaknesses, so you can balance each other out and learn from each other. Another group member may provide a catalyst for you for a great spiritual discovery. Each member also has different experiences to bring to the mix. One may have studied Celtic mythology, and another Greek. Everyone is a resource. Being in a group can motivate you too. It's hard to slack if you have others to answer to. Most important, it's hard to learn a mystery religion in a vacuum.

Disadvantages of Group Work

The downside of group work is that you can't do everything you want, whenever you want, without taking another person's opinion or preferences into account. You may have to deal with egos, politics, and personality clashes. You may have one member who uses or pushes around the others. You may have members who don't do their share of the work, show up late to meetings, don't contribute to the materials you need, and generally leech off the rest of the group. You have to plan your meetings and rituals around other people's schedules. You might disagree about what deities you'd like to work with, how you'd like to cast the circle, whether you'll have white or red wine, and just about everything else.

Deciding whether to work in a group or fly solo is a difficult choice. Remember, though, that you can always change your mind later. If you join a group, you can leave it. If you decide to work alone for a while, you can join a group later. Many Wiccans fluctuate between group and solitary work depending on their schedules, access to others, and where they are on their spiritual path. Neither way is necessarily better than the other.

If I Don't Want to Work Alone, What Are My Options?

Work with a Friend or Start Your Own Group

One of the easiest ways to explore Wicca with others is to find a friend or two who are also interested in Wicca and work together as a small group. If you start with friends, it's likely that you'll be comfortable, and your small group can provide a safe space for all of you to learn about Wicca. Starting your own group can be a lot of work, but with only a few members it's easier, and you can split the planning, writing, and prop-gathering between you. If you work successfully in your small group for a while, you may decide you want to take in new members, and your small group might grow into a coven. There is no set minimum or maximum number of members for a coven, although many Wiccans I know believe you need at least three people. A one-member coven seems a tad ridiculous though.

Join an Established Coven or Group

Another option is to look for an existing coven and petition to join it. Depending on where you live, this may or may not be possible for you. Each coven will have its own rules about who can join and when. Some start teaching new people at the beginning of the year, so they only take on students then. Others have an open-door policy, and people drop in and out as they see fit. Still others require applications and for the petitioner to meet with the group one or more times beforehand to make sure everyone is comfortable and compatible. Many covens will vote on new members before allowing them to join. This, again, is to make sure that everyone is comfortable. No coven has to take you on if they don't want to. A word of caution: If a group doesn't take its member policy seriously, it may be a group you will not be comfortable joining. In my experience, many new Wiccans like to feel "safe" until they get the hang of things, and if people are coming and going all the time, it's hard to get the stability you may need. In addition, if the member policy is very loose, the group may be disorganized and there may be no protocol for behavior. This can make for a very free and uplifting experience, or a frustrating, disrespectful one, depending on the group.

Attend Open Public Rituals

Finding open rituals can be difficult if you live in a rural area, but many cities have at least one Wiccan group that puts on public ritual, and there are more and more open rural groups springing up. The advantages of open ritual are that the circles often are different each time, and someone else has done the work and planning, so you can just go, enjoy, and learn. It's a good way to meet other Wiccans in your area, and maybe even find members of a coven you'd like to join. (Although covens have their own private rituals, members may also attend public rituals for the social aspect, to look for potential members or students, or just to see how someone else does things.) The downside is that most of the time these rituals aren't meant to be anyone's sole source of religious practice, and the groups that put them on are performing a community service rather than starting a "church," so there may not be much continuity. Since the rituals are open, you also have no control over who shows up and who doesn't. If you're surrounded by strangers, you may not feel like you can really get comfortable and into the ritual.

Study with a Teacher

Finding a teacher may or may not be the same as seeking out a coven because some teachers lead covens and others don't. Some covens are "teaching covens," and students are allowed to become members after studying with the teacher for a while. Some teachers take on individual students, and others will take on small numbers of students for a period of time. In this last case, at the end of the training, the student moves on rather than joining a group.

If you are studying with a teacher, whether it is solo, in a class, or as part of a training coven, it's likely that you'll be asked to do a certain number of assignments, including reading books from a specific list, writing or journaling about your experiences, energy exercises, studying mythology and the gods, and learning about ethics, magic, and creating and performing ritual. There may or may not be a test or tests. As with teachers of all subjects, some teachers are very hands-off, and others are deeply involved in their students' process. Some will want to meet with you regularly, and others will not. Some will have you work at your own pace, and others will have a schedule.

Attend Wicca Classes

Attending Wicca classes is different than working with a teacher. They are usually open classes held in a public place, such as a bookstore. If you have a metaphysical bookstore nearby, check there to see if they offer classes, or know anyone who does. Wicca classes held in stores are often informal, and the quality varies from great to lousy. Even if the class is less than inspiring, however, it can be a way to learn about Wiccan resources in your community. Wicca classes are often inexpensive or free. Many Wiccan traditions believe that it is wrong to take money for teaching the Craft, in which case the teacher will not charge or will charge just enough to cover the cost of renting the class space.

Join a Wiccan Student Group

If you are in college, there may be a Wiccan student group on your campus. If you join, you can meet like-minded people on campus to work with and learn from. If there isn't a Wiccan group, you can start one, but if you do this, go into it with your eyes open. It's a lot of work—rewarding work, but time-consuming nevertheless. Years ago, a friend of mine and I started a group at our university. The group met every other week, and frequently we had speakers from different Wiccan and pagan groups in the area. The best part about it was that while providing this service to others, my friend and I could meet and "audition" the local Wiccan leaders who came to speak and find out who we wanted to learn more about. We also became much better ritual leaders because the majority of the work fell on our shoulders. One thing you must take into account if you decide to do this is that starting a Wiccan group on campus, no matter how large your school is, makes you a public Wiccan figure. When my friend and I were leading the student group, we got more than our fair share of attention from the fundamentalist religious student groups, and there were times when it was very uncomfortable. If you've got a thick skin and some support, though, I can attest that starting your own student group is worth the work.

Join an Online Coven or Email List

If you can't find a group you like by any of the conventional means already mentioned, you might consider joining an online coven. These can't provide face-to-face practice and teaching, but they do offer support and resources.

Email lists can hold a wealth of information too. You can join them through Yahoo Groups and other similar services. There is also a collection of links to email lists on *The Witches' Voice* Web site, www.witchvox.com. You can network on email lists, ask questions, compare practice, find out where to get tools, and much more. Remember, though, that as with anything on the Internet, some of the information you'll receive will be great, and some will be wrong, bad, or ridiculous, so exercise some caution.

How Do I Find a Group?

Surf the Internet

Whether or not you can find a group in your area will depend on where you live. The easiest, and possibly the best, resource for finding a group is *The Witches' Voice* Web site. There is a large section of the site dedicated to listing groups and classes from all over the country. You can click on your state and search the list for your city or town. You can also put the name of your city or town and the word "Wicca" in an Internet search engine and see what comes up. Some covens and groups have their own Web sites. Avoid any group that tries to sell you an expensive book of shadows or online Wicca courses. Most of the groups who offer these things are just out to make a quick buck, and the quality of the material you receive is very poor, if you get it at all. Don't forget to ask about groups in your area on your email lists too.

Check Pagan Publications

If there is a new age or pagan paper in your area, that's a good place to look too, as are Wiccan magazines. You can subscribe online to some Wiccan magazines if you can't find them in your local stores.

Network

Another good way to find groups is to ask around, especially at metaphysical bookstores. Ask friends. Ask the woman wearing the pentagram on the bus. Ask the guy at the coffee shop reading the book about Greek mythology. The last time I was at a coffee shop, there was a woman sitting in the corner reading someone's astrological chart off of her laptop. Based on her large collection of silver rings with magical symbols on them, I'm guessing she was Wiccan.

Sometimes you will see postings at what we fondly call "hippie havens," aka co-ops, health food stores, herb shops, colleges, coffee shops, art fairs, crystal and rock shops, and yoga studios. Unitarian churches or interfaith councils may also be good resources. If you have a local Goth club, Renaissance festival or medieval faire, Irish heritage festival, Irish pub, belly dance class, drumming circle, science fiction convention, or chapter of the SCA (Society for Creative Anachronism; a group that studies and re-creates the Middle Ages), I can almost guarantee that it will be a hotbed of Wiccan and pagan activity. Don't let the fangs, kilts, Spock ears, and homemade broadswords scare you away. It's quite possible that these folks can help you find what you're looking for.

Are There Particular Things I Should Look for in a Group?

Before joining any group, see if you can check them out by asking around in person or on an email list and visiting their Web site (if they have one). Get a read on the group's reputation in the community. Unfortunately, it is quite likely that you'll hear a lot of gossip if you do this, and that can be very disheartening. Check out any rumors rather than believing them without question. Oftentimes they spring out of honest misunderstandings, but there is malicious gossip in the Wiccan community too. In my opinion it's better to hear the gossip and chase down the truth about it than to go into a new group blind.

Here are some questions to ask yourself or your potential coven mates.

COMFORT LEVEL. When you meet the members, do you have any negative reactions to any of them? Do any warning bells go off? Do they seem to respect each other? Can you sense tensions in the group? Ask questions and take time to get to know them a bit before leaping in.

ETHICS. Do you feel that the group has a positive focus? Do they follow the Wiccan Rede or some similar ethical code? Do members of the group bad-mouth each other or members of other groups?

PHILOSOPHY. Is their interpretation of Wicca in line with yours?

EXPECTATIONS. Has the group clearly laid out their expectations of members, and do they follow those guidelines? Do they have a code or rules about how they treat each other? Are you expected to put in a certain amount of time? Is there a set of requirements that you must fulfill in order to join? Are you expected to contribute items such as candles and food to the group? Are you expected to pay money to attend the group? If so, is the money just to cover costs of ritual materials, or is it for something else? (This is a potential red flag.)

SCHEDULE. Does the group's schedule fit yours? Some groups are very time-intensive, so if you're in school or you have a family, you may need to find a group that meets less often.

STRUCTURE. Is the group structured or freeform? Who is in charge? How are decisions made? Is responsibility shared? Is it a democracy, a dictatorship, or something else, and can you live with it, whatever it is?

STYLE. Style is really a mixture of comfort level and structure. Is the group fond of large, theatrical ritual or quieter circles? Is it focused on serious study, fun, partying, magical work, ritual work, or all of the above? Do they wear robes, street clothes, ritual wear, or go skyclad? Do some of their rituals include sex or sexual symbolism, and if so, are you okay with that?

FLAVOR. Does the group follow a particular tradition, cultural background, or set of gods, or does it pull from many different sources? In other words, are they traditional or eclectic? If they say they follow an established tradition, is there a way to check that they are who they say they are and they do what they say they do?

What Do "Eclectic" and "Traditional" Mean, and What's the Difference?

Most Wiccan practice can be divided into two categories: eclectic and traditional. Viewpoints on the definitions of these two terms vary, but in general, eclectic Wiccans compile their practices from a variety of sources, and traditional Wiccans use a system of practices handed down to them by someone else and that have a certain level of consistency. The lines blur in some places because there are Wiccans who call themselves members of a tradition, but they cull practices from different sources. Although they pick and choose, groups like these often have some point of continuity, such as working only with the Celtic gods or using a specific format for their circles, even if the individual parts of the ritual change.

Should I Be an Eclectic Wiccan or a Traditional One?

The answer to this question, as with many of these questions, will depend on your preferences and the options and resources available to you. You might decide, for example, that structure is important to you and look for a group of Wiccans that practice a structured tradition, but there may not be one in your area. For the sake of argument, let's say that you have access to every kind of group possible. Then you choose based on where someone with your needs and habits will flourish the most.

Eclectic Wiccans have a great deal of freedom. They can take ritual elements that they like from books, open rituals, friends, and online sources and disregard the parts they don't want to use. They can make up rituals on the spot or plan elaborate rites. They can practice alone or in groups. They answer to no one, and their rituals can be tailored perfectly to suit their needs. They are empowered to teach themselves and build their own path, even if they work with a group. That's powerful stuff.

When you teach yourself Wicca, however, as opposed to learning a single cohesive system from someone else, there may be things that you miss. It's hard to know that you don't know something if you don't have a person or traditional framework to make that apparent. If you're learning a tradition, chances are you're receiving your training in a more cohesive and systematic way. Most eclectic Wiccans also miss out on one of the coolest things in Wicca, or any religion for that matter—being able to tap into the egregore, or collective energy of everyone who has practiced a particular ritual. When a rite is practiced over and over again across time, it develops a power of its own. When you do the ritual, you plug into that energy source. Instantly, you are connected to everyone else who follows that tradition and does that ritual. You can experience this easily in a Catholic church. The buildings hum with the energy of repeated ritual. If you create new rituals every time and do them only once, you don't tap into the collective as easily.

Structured training and tapping the egregore are two of the positive aspects of practicing traditional Wicca. Other pluses are that since you don't have to write rituals every time, you have more energy to devote to just experiencing the rites. In this way, the structure is freeing. The consistent elements become psychic triggers that can bring you quickly into ritual "head space." Because you repeat the rites, they begin to take on layers of significance that they can't if you only do them once. If you do the same rites for several years, you begin to see different things in them. The energy in circle flows well because all of the parts and pieces were created to fit together. In addition, as a traditional Wiccan you not only have the support of your group, you also can connect with other members of the tradition across the globe (if your tradition is international). If you practice a family tradition, you have the added bonus of being able to tap into your bloodline.

The downside of traditional practice is its lack of spontaneity. Although there may be freedom within the structure, there is still a structure. Many people come to Wicca to escape structured religion. There is also often a hierarchy in traditional Wicca, with those who know the most about the tradition "outranking" those who know less. Traditional Wicca has to work this way because if you're passing on a tradition, you necessarily know more about it than the person you're passing it to, at least until you've passed the whole thing. There are also a lot of rules in traditional Wicca, and you have little to no say in creating them. Wiccans, as I've noted, don't take well to others telling them what to do, which is one reason eclectic practice is so popular. There's also the family factor. When you are part of a tradition, you have the support and shared experience of others in the tradition, but you also have to deal with the tradition's politics and personalities.

For those interested in looking into traditional practice, here is a partial list of Wiccan traditions. Because of limited space, I am not doing any of these traditions justice, but this should give you a taste that might inspire you to explore one or more of the traditions further.

Gardnerian

The Gardnerian tradition descends from Gerald Gardner, who is mentioned earlier in this book. Gardnerianism is probably the oldest Wiccan tradition in the United States, excluding folk and family traditions. It jumped the pond from England in the 1960s. It is a very structured, hierarchical, mystery tradition. It has three degrees, or levels of study. It is also an initiatory tradition, which means to become Gardnerian you have to be "made" Gardnerian by another Gardnerian in a specific ceremony. Gardnerianism has a lineage, which is a kind of family tree that tells who initiated whom into the tradition. Its rites and the contents of its book of shadows are oathbound, which means they are secret and can only be revealed to other Gardnerians. Gardnerians worship skyclad and observe the eight sabbats.

Alexandrian

The Alexandrian tradition follows the work of Alex Sanders. Sanders was initiated as a witch in the early 1960s. He was also a ceremonial magician, which influenced some of the tradition's practices. The Alexandrian tradition has a lot in common with the Gardnerian tradition. Alexandrians observe the eight sabbats, have a three-degree hierarchy, and may worship either robed or skyclad. Alexandrianism is also an oathbound, lineaged, initiatory tradition.

Feri

The Feri tradition was established by Victor and Cora Anderson in the early 1970s. The Andersons had experience with a wide variety of pagan practices, and they melded them into the new tradition. Among other things, Feri has roots in Appalachian magic. Feri is an initiatory tradition, but there is only one degree. Some of its material is oathbound. Its members work both in covens and as solitaries, and they observe the eight sabbats.

1734

1734 is a tradition culled from a set of letters written by Robert Cochrane, who was magister of the Clan of Tubal Cain in the United Kingdom. Cochrane had a broad knowledge of folk practices of Great Britain, some of which he communicated in the letters, which were part of a series of correspondence from the 1960s between Cochrane and an American named Joseph Wilson. They do not detail an entire tradition, however, so 1734 practitioners have filled in the gaps with practices from other Wiccan traditions. There is no lineage, book of shadows, or initiation. 1734 does not refer to a year. It is, in Cochrane's words, a number that "meant something to a witch."

Celtic and/or Celtic Reconstructionist

Celtic Reconstructionist Wicca is Wicca that focuses on deities and practices primarily from Ireland, Scotland, and the other Celtic countries. Since most of the pagan Celtic practices have been lost, Celtic Wiccans research history and literature of the Celtic countries to try to re-create some of these practices and incorporate them into Wicca. Celtic Wicca is most often an eclectic path, although there are new Celtic Wiccan traditions being created. One common theme among Celtic Reconstructionists is that they work with the "three realms"—sky, land, and sea—instead of the four elements. Most of them observe the four major sabbats—Samhain, Imbolc, Beltane, and Lammas—but there is no central structure, lineage, or oathbound material. There are also Greek and Norse Reconstructionists who seek to do something similar, except in the framework of those cultures.

Minoan

The Minoan tradition was created in 1977 and is based on the ancient civilizations of the Mediterranean, especially those of Crete. It has three separate branches: the Minoan Sisterhood for women, the Minoan Brotherhood for men, and the Cult of Rhea for both. It is an oathbound, initiatory tradition with Gardnerian influences.

Seax Wicca

Seax Wicca was created by Raymond Buckland in 1974. Buckland is credited with bringing Gardnerian Wicca to the United States, but Seax Wicca is not related to Gardnerianism. Seax Wicca borrows from many sources, central being the Saxon and Norse traditions. Its primary deities are Woden and Freya, with Woden presiding over the dark half of the year, from Samhain to Beltane, and Freya over the light half, from Beltane to Samhain. Seax covens are autonomous and democratic, and their material is not oathbound. Seax Wicca recognizes self-initiation, where the dedicant declares himself or herself Wiccan rather than being "made" Wiccan by someone else.

Asatru

Asatru is not Wicca in the strictest sense, but the two practices overlap in several places and Asatru has become popular, so I am including it here. Asatru is a tradition based on the Norse Eddas and other sources. It was established in the United States in 1973, but its roots are in Iceland. Its priests are called gothi and its priestesses gythia. Asatru practitioners work with the Norse gods. They do not necessarily observe the eight sabbats, although many of them mark Yule and Ostara. Some also observe a holiday called Winternights, which occurs in the fall. Asatru is not an oathbound tradition.

Church of All Worlds (CAW)

The Church of All Worlds is one of the first fully incorporated neopagan churches. It was created in 1962 by a group of friends who were inspired by Robert Heinlein's novel *Stranger in a Strange Land*. The central ritual that CAW groups practice is called "water sharing." This ritual acknowledges the divine within those sharing the water. Many groups are members of CAW, but they vary widely in practice. Generally they observe the eight sabbats.

Covenant of the Goddess (COG)

COG is not a tradition per se, but rather an umbrella group that was created in 1975 in order to give Wiccans and pagans legal protection and legitimate ministerial credentials. COG is made up of autonomous covens and solitary Wiccans, but all members agree to a common code of ethics.

New Reformed Orthodox Order of the Golden Dawn (NROOGD)

NROOGD was created by a student at San Francisco State University as part of a class assignment, but it quickly took on an energy of its own and spread. It has a central liturgy, it recognizes a god and a triple goddess, and its members work skyclad.

Central Valley Wicca (CVW)

Central Valley Wicca is actually a group of traditions—including the Kingstone, Silver Crescent, Daoine Coire, Majestic, and Assembly of Wicca—that came out of the Central Valley area of California. There is some dispute about how Wicca got there in the first place, and thus also about the origin of these traditions, but some practitioners trace it back to a woman from the United Kingdom who may have relocated to the area in the 1960s. Kingstone is probably the largest of the CVW traditions. Its practices are similar in some respects to Gardnerianism, and it is an oathbound initiatory tradition with a core book of shadows. Kingstones observe the eight sabbats.

Blue Star

Blue Star Wicca was started in 1975 by Frank Dufner, but it was spread largely by his wife, Tzipora, and her second husband, Kenny Klein, who were traveling musicians. Blue Star is a hierarchical, oathbound tradition with roots in Alexandrianism. It observes the eight sabbats.

Dianic Wicca

Dianic Wicca arose from the feminist movement. In 1976, Zsuzsanna Budapest wrote a book called *The Feminist Book of Lights and Shadows*, which became the core text for the tradition. The book has since been republished as the *Holy Book of Women's Mysteries*. Dianic Wiccans practice in all-female circles and worship only female divinity.

Reclaiming

The Reclaiming tradition has a strong environmental and activist focus, and it seeks to fuse politics and spirituality. It developed out of the Reclaiming Collective, a group of feminists that in turn came out of classes created by Starhawk and Diane Baker in 1978. Starhawk is the author of *The Spiral Dance*, one of the most popular books ever written about Wicca. There is no hierarchy or core belief structure in the tradition, but its members agree to adhere to the group's "Principles of Unity." Groups are run by consensus.

So which is better, eclectic or traditional? The answer is that Wiccans are lucky to have both options, and whichever one works for you is the one that's better. For you. I practiced as an eclectic for a decade and then decided I wanted to fill in the gaps in my knowledge with formal training. I joined a tradition and went through the degrees, and now I teach that tradition. Being a traditional Wiccan has brought me to some places in my life that I may never have found otherwise, but I wouldn't be the Wiccan I am if I hadn't first explored and experimented as an eclectic. My coven is about as traditional as they get. My private practice—the personal stuff I do without my coven—is eclectic and not traditional at all. So you could say I'm cheating, but there are no rules that say I can't, as long as I don't mix my eclectic practices in with my traditional ones. You can have your cake and eat it too, if that is what serves your spiritual purpose and helps you walk the path of the gods.

Are There Particular Things I Should Look For in a Teacher?

When looking for a teacher, you should ask most of the same questions I listed for looking for a group, and ask for references. Talk to the potential teacher's other students, if possible. Ask around about him or her in the community, bearing in mind the gossip factor, and plug his or her name into an Internet search engine and see what comes up. If the teacher has teachers or elders, ask if you can speak to them as well. Some teachers may find this insulting, but ask anyway—respectfully. The elders may not be able to tell you much if the teacher's tradition is oathbound, and the teacher may not be able to reveal who his or her elders are because that's oathbound, but it's worth trying. Most importantly, as with looking for a group, tell the teacher what you are looking for and what your philosophy is so together you can determine if he or she is the right fit for you.

Most Wiccan teachers are honest, ethical, well-meaning folk, but there are some people who pose as Wiccan teachers in order to take advantage of others, offering "training" for money or sex. It is not unheard of to ask for money for training, so don't let that stop you if you've found a teacher you like, and don't assume that because the teacher charges that he or she is a fraud. However, the amount should be stated up front and be reasonable. As I said earlier, there are many, many traditions that forbid taking money for teaching. The teacher was given the gift of the knowledge by his or her teacher, and now is passing along the knowledge. As for sex, if a teacher insists on it, get out and don't look back. As I've already established, there are some Wiccan traditions that include ritual sex, and Wiccans see sex as sacred, but ritual sex and sex as payment for instruction are not the same thing. The latter is unethical at best.

Am I a Real Wiccan if I Don't Have a Teacher or a Tradition?

Does it take a Wiccan to make a Wiccan? Are you a Wiccan just because you decide that you are? In other words, do you have to find a teacher and go through formal training to become Wiccan, or do you just have to study and dedicate yourself to the path? If you ever feel like starting a fistfight at a large Wiccan gathering, opening up a debate about these questions would be a good way to do it. Some Wiccans feel that you're not truly Wiccan unless you have been trained. Some Wiccans would rather eat broken glass than go through someone else's idea of training or practice someone else's way. And some potential Wiccans want training, but can't find it in their area. Should they be barred from calling themselves Wiccan just because they can't find anyone to teach them?

If you read the list of traditions, you'll notice that several of them are initiatory, for example the Gardnerian, Alexandrian, and Feri. That means that you can't declare that you're a Gardnerian, Alexandrian, or Feri unless you have been "brought in" by a legitimate member of that tradition. (By the way, claiming to be initiated into a tradition when you haven't is very, very disrespectful, and bad Wiccan etiquette, not to mention a lie.) However, that doesn't necessarily mean you can't be a legitimate Wiccan without initiation. And you can definitely be a witch without initiation. You can join several of the traditions or groups on the list without being initiated, and you can practice solitary too. There are plenty of self-identified Wiccans and witches out there practicing happily without the benefit of being deemed a Wiccan by someone else.

You should know, though, that some Wiccans won't consider you Wiccan unless you have undergone an initiation ceremony of some kind. This is not because they are elitist, exclusive snobs—the country-club set of the Wiccan community.

There are legitimate reasons for the belief that you need initiation. First, some believe that it's impossible to teach yourself a complete and cohesive religious system. As I said before, if you haven't been trained or you're not working in a specific framework, you might miss something because you aren't aware of what you don't know. Another reason some Wiccans believe that you must be initiated is that they see Wicca as a mystery tradition. Mystery traditions are designed to help you have a certain set of experiences and revelations in a certain order. This is not something you can do for yourself. My tradition is a mystery tradition, and I can tell you that there is no way my initiation experience would have revealed to me the things it did had I done it alone. (Actually, it's impossible to do it alone, but for the sake of argument let's say that I could have.) That said, I believe that if you really work the Wiccan system, you will have your own revelations and experiences of the mysteries over time.

There are also Wiccans who believe that the word Wiccan should apply only to witches who belong to traditions that have descended from Gerald Gardner because he popularized the term, and to him it referred to the teachings he was given as opposed to witchcraft in general. People who hold this belief usually think that everyone not "related" to Gardner should use the term witch instead of Wiccan. In the United States, we call the traditions derived from Gardner "British Traditional Witchcraft," although that phrase means something else entirely in the United Kingdom. Others believe that the toothpaste is out of the tube, so to speak, and the word is no longer associated solely with British Traditional Witchcraft, so any witch who wants to can call him- or herself Wiccan.

As you can see, the issue of "what makes a Wiccan" is complex. The question, then, is whether you believe you can be Wiccan without initiation, whether you feel the term applies to you ("witch" is a perfectly good word too, after all), and whether the opinions of those other Wiccans matter to you.

Wicca is many things, but above all it is a path of empowerment. It stands to reason, then, that you should be able to declare yourself Wiccan or create your own self-initiation ceremony. This can be a personal rite that you do alone, or you can do it with friends or your coven. There are ideas for self-initiations in many Wicca books and online, and you can use them or dream up something that is only yours. One can argue that a ritual you create yourself—a rite that truly gets to the heart of your desire to be a Wiccan or witch—can be as powerful and transformative as any rite anyone else can put you through, if not more so.

Some Wiccans choose to do a dedication ritual instead of a self-initiation. This puts their feet on their new path without having to deal with the "valid initiation" issue. Nobody can question your dedication if you do it in a heartfelt way and make a commitment. After all, when you strip away all the trappings, the opinions of others, the rules, and traditions, Wicca is just you and the gods, and a dedication is a promise to yourself and to them.

If you do a self-initiation or dedication, the gods and your subconscious both will take you seriously and begin to make it a reality, so do it with respect. Don't stop with an initiation or dedication—it is a beginning, not an ending. Study, work the path, and continue to learn. Don't become a one-book wonder, an insta-Wiccan, or a fluff bunny. Whether you initiate yourself or someone does it for you, you are saying to the gods and—more importantly—to yourself, "Here I am! I will know the gods. I will discover the mysteries. I will work actively and spiritually to develop as a person." You are beginning to find and work your true will. It's as simple and complex as that, and so mote it be.

Further Reading

Note: The editions listed below are not necessarily the oldest or the most recent; they're the ones sitting on my bookshelf. There may be other editions available. Some of them may also be out of print. Check your local used bookstore or online sources (such as Abe Books) for copies. For British editions that are difficult to find in the United States, try Amazon.com.uk.

Basic Wicca and Paganism Books

Adler, Margot. *Drawing Down the Moon*. Boston: Beacon Press, 1979.

Buckland, Raymond. *Buckland's Complete Book of Witchcraft*. St. Paul, MN: Llewellyn Publications, 1993.

Coyle, T. Thorn. *Evolutionary Witchcraft*. New York: Penguin, 2004.

Crowley, Vivianne. *Way of Wicca*. London: Thorsons, 1997.

———. *Wicca*. London: Thorsons, 1996.

Crowther, Patricia. *Lid off the Cauldron*. Somerset, England: Capall Bann, 1998.

Cunningham, Scott. *Living Wicca: A Further Guide for the Solitary Practitioner*. St. Paul, MN: Llewellyn Publications, 1997.

———. *Wicca: A Guide for the Solitary Practitioner*. St. Paul, MN: Llewellyn Publications, 1989.

Farrar, Janet and Stewart. *Eight Sabbats for Witches*. Custer, WA: Phoenix Publishing, 1981.

———. *A Witches' Bible: The Complete Witches' Handbook*. Custer, WA: Phoenix Publishing, 1981.

Fitch, Ed. *A Grimoire of Shadows*. St. Paul, MN: Llewellyn Publications, 2001.

Gardner, Gerald B. *The Meaning of Witchcraft*. Lake Toxaway, NC: Mercury Press, 1999.

———. *Witchcraft Today*. Lake Toxaway, NC: Mercury Press, 1999.

K., Amber. *Covencraft: Witchcraft for Three or More*. St. Paul, MN: Llewellyn Publications, 1998.

Martello, Dr. Leo Louis. *Witchcraft: The Old Religion*. Secaucus, NJ: Citadel Press, 1974.

Starhawk. *The Spiral Dance*. San Francisco: Harper & Row, 1979.

Valiente, Doreen. *An ABC of Witchcraft*. Custer, WA: Phoenix Publishing, 1973.

———. *Natural Magic*. Custer, WA: Phoenix Publishing, 1975.

———. *The Rebirth of Witchcraft*. Custer, WA: Phoenix Publishing, 1989.

———. *Witchcraft for Tomorrow*. Custer, WA: Phoenix Publishing, 1978.

Zimmerman, Denise, and Katherine A. Gleason. *The Complete Idiot's Guide to Wicca and Witchcraft*. Indianapolis, IN: Alpha Books, 2000.

Wicca-Related Subjects

Animal Familiars

Andrews, Ted. *Animal Speak*. St. Paul, MN: Llewellyn Publications, 1993.

Smith, Penelope. *Animal Talk: Interspecies Telepathic Communication*. Hillsboro, OR: Beyond Words Publishing, 1999.

Folklore

Evans-Wentz, W. Y. *The Fairy Faith in Celtic Countries*. New York: Citadel Press, 1990.

Frazer, Sir James. *The Golden Bough*. 1922. Reprint, London: Penguin Books, 1996.

Graves, Robert. *The White Goddess*. New York: Farrar, Strauss, and Giroux, 1975.

McNeill, Marian F. *The Silver Bough, Volumes 1–4*. Glasgow: Beith Printing Co., 1990.

The Goddess and God

Baring, Anne, and Jules Cashford. *The Myth of the Goddess: Evolution of an Image*. London: Penguin, 1991.

Farrar, Janet and Stewart. *The Witches' Goddess*. Custer, WA: Phoenix Publishing, 1987.

Fitch, Eric L. *In Search of Herne the Hunter*. Somerset, England: Capall Bann, 1994.

Jackson, Nigel Aldcroft. *Call of the Horned Piper*. Somerset, England: Capall Bann, 1994.

———. *Masks of Misrule*. Somerset, England: Capall Bann, 1996.

Monaghan, Patricia. *The Book of Goddesses and Heroines*. St. Paul, MN: Llewellyn Publications, 1990.

———. *The Goddess Companion: Daily Meditations on the Feminine Spirit*. St. Paul, MN: Llewellyn Publications, 1999.

———. *The Goddess Path: Myths, Invocations, and Rituals*. St. Paul, MN: Llewellyn Publications, 1999.

Neumann, Erich. *The Great Mother: An Analysis of the Archetype*. Princeton, NJ: Princeton University Press, 1983.

Herbs, Incense, and Oils

Beyerl, Paul. *A Compendium of Herbal Magick.* Custer, WA: Phoenix Publishing, 1998.

Cech, Richo. *Making Plant Medicine.* Williams, OR: Horizon Herbs, LLC, 2000.

Culpeper, Nicholas. *Culpeper's Complete Herbal.* Avon: The Bath Press, 1998. Note: There are many versions of *Culpeper's Herbal* in print, including more extensive ones than this edition.

Cunningham, Scott. *Cunningham's Encyclopedia of Magical Herbs.* St. Paul, MN: Llewellyn Publications, 1985.

———. *Magical Herbalism.* St. Paul, MN: Llewellyn Publications, 1991.

———. *The Magic of Incense, Oils, and Brews.* St. Paul, MN: Llewellyn Publications, 1988.

Griffin, Judy. *Mother Nature's Herbal.* St. Paul, MN: Llewellyn Publications, 1997.

Williams, Jude. *Jude's Herbal Home Remedies.* Llewellyn Publications, 1992.

Wylundt. *Wylundt's Book of Incense.* York Beach, ME: Weiser Books, 1996.

History of Paganism, Witchcraft, and Wicca

Baroja, Julio Caro. *The World of the Witches.* London: Phoenix Press, 2001.

Guiley, Rosemary Ellen. *The Encyclopedia of Witches and Witchcraft*. New York: Facts on File, 1989.

Ginzburg, Carlo. *Ecstasies: Deciphering the Witches' Sabbath*. New York: Penguin, 1991.

———. *The Night Battles*. Baltimore: Johns Hopkins University Press, 1992.

Heselton, Philip. *Gerald Gardner and the Cauldron of Inspiration*. Somerset, England: Capall Bann, 2003.

———. *Wiccan Roots: Gerald Gardner and the Modern Witchcraft Revival*. Somerset, England: Capall Bann, 2000.

Hole, Christina. *Witchcraft in England*. New York: Charles Scribner's Sons, 1947.

Hutton, Ronald. *The Triumph of the Moon: A History of Modern Pagan Witchcraft*. London: Oxford University Press, 1999.

Jones, Prudence, and Nigel Pennick. *A History of Pagan Europe*. London: Routledge, 1995.

Murray, Margaret. *The God of the Witches*. London: Oxford University Press, 1952.

———. *The Witch-Cult in Western Europe*. London: Oxford University Press, 1922.

Ross, Anne. *Pagan Celtic Britain*. Chicago: Academy Chicago Publishers, 1967.

Magic and Correspondences

Bills, Rex. *The Rulership Book*. Tempe, AZ: American Federation of Astrologers, 1971.

Bonewits, Isaac. *Real Magic*. York Beach, ME: Samuel Weiser, 1989.

Crowley, Aleister. *Magick in Theory and Practice*. New York: Magickal Childe Publishing, 1990.

Daniels, Estelle. *Astrologickal Magick*. York Beach, ME: Samuel Weiser, 1995.

Duquette, Lon Milo. *The Chicken Qabalah of Rabbi Lamed Ben Clifford*. York Beach, ME: Samuel Weiser, 2001.

———. *The Magick of Aleister Crowley: A Handbook of the Rituals of Thelema*. York Beach, ME: Samuel Weiser, 2003.

Kraig, Donald Michael. *Modern Magick*. St. Paul, MN: Llewellyn Publications, 1993.

Simms, Maria Kay. *A Time for Magick*. St. Paul, MN: Llewellyn Publications, 2001.

Mystery Traditions

Kerenyi, Carl. *Eleusis: Archetypal Image of Mother and Daughter*. Princeton, NJ: Princeton University Press, 1967.

Meyer, Marvin W. *The Ancient Mysteries: A Sourcebook of Sacred Texts*. Philadelphia: University of Pennsylvania Press, 1987.

Stewart, R. J. *The Underworld Initiation*. Chapel Hill, NC: Mercury Publishing, 1990.

Mythology

Campbell, Joseph. *The Hero with a Thousand Faces*. Princeton, NJ: Princeton University Press, 1968.

———. *The Mythic Image*. Princeton, NJ: Princeton University Press, 1974.

———. *Myths to Live By*. New York: Penguin, 1972.

———. *The Power of Myth*. DVD. Apostrophe S Productions, 1988. Distributed most recently by Mystic Fire Video.

———. *The Power of Myth*. New York: Doubleday, 1988.

———. *Transformation of Myth Through Time*. New York: Harper & Row, 1990.

Shamanism

Eliade, Mircea. *Shamanism: Archaic Techniques of Ecstasy*. Princeton, NJ: University of Princeton Press, 1964.

Johnson, Kenneth. *North Star Road*. St. Paul, MN: Llewellyn Publications, 1996.

Kalweit, Holger. *Dreamtime and Inner Space: The World of the Shaman*. Boston: Shambhala, 1984.

Matthews, Caitlin. *Singing the Soul Back Home: Shamanism in Daily Life*. Shaftsbury, Dorset, England: Element Books, 1995.

Stones and Crystals

Cunningham, Scott. *Cunningham's Encyclopedia of Crystal, Gem, and Metal Magic*. St. Paul, MN: Llewellyn Publications, 1993.

Melody. *Love Is in the Earth: A Kaleidoscope of Crystals.* Wheat Ridge, CO: Earth-Love Publishing House, 1995.

Unconscious, Conscious, and Psychic Stuff

Glass, Justine. *Witchcraft: The Sixth Sense*. North Hollywood, CA: Wilshire Book Co., 1965.

Hillman, James. *The Dream and the Underworld.* New York: Harper & Row, 1979.

Roth, Gabrielle. *Sweat Your Prayers*. New York: J. P. Tarcher/Putnam, 1997.

Swann, Ingo. *Everybody's Guide to Natural ESP*. Los Angeles: Jeremy P. Tarcher, Inc., 1991.

Index

N

O

P

To Write to the Author

If you wish to contact the author or would like more information about this book, please write to the author in care of Llewellyn Worldwide and we will forward your request. Both the author and publisher appreciate hearing from you and learning of your enjoyment of this book and how it has helped you. Llewellyn Worldwide cannot guarantee that every letter written to the author can be answered, but all will be forwarded. Please write to:

Thea Sabin
% Llewellyn Worldwide
2143 Wooddale Drive, Dept. 0-7387-0751-1
Woodbury, MN 55125-2989

Please enclose a self-addressed stamped envelope for reply, or $1.00 to cover costs. If outside U.S.A., enclose international postal reply coupon.

Many of Llewellyn's authors have websites with additional information and resources. For more information, please visit our website:

WWW.LLEWELLYN.COM

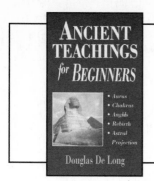

Aura Reading for Beginners

Develop Your Psychic Awareness for Health & Success

RICHARD WEBSTER

When you lose your temper, don't be surprised if a dirty red haze suddenly appears around you. If you do something magnanimous, your aura will expand. Now you can learn to see the energy that emanates off yourself and other people through the proven methods taught by Richard Webster in his psychic training classes.

Learn to feel the aura, see the colors in it, and interpret what those colors mean. Explore the chakra system, and how to restore balance to chakras that are over- or under-stimulated. Then you can begin to imprint your desires into your aura to attract what you want in your life.

1-56718-798-6, 208 pp., 5 3/16 x 8, illus. $9.95

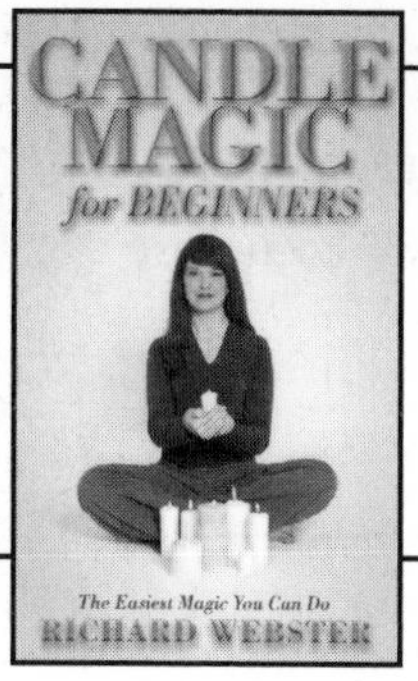

Candle Magic for Beginners

Richard Webster

Anyone who has made a wish before blowing out birthday candles has practiced candle magic. Quick, easy, and effective, this magical art requires no religious doctrine or previous magic experience. Anyone can practice candle magic and Richard Webster shows you how to get started. Learn how to perform rituals, spells, and divinations to gain luck, love, prosperity, protection, healing, and happiness. Also included are tips for which kinds of candles to use, candle maintenance and preparation, best times for magic, and how to make your own candles.

0-7387-0535-7, 312 pp., 5$\frac{3}{16}$ x 8 **$12.95**

Divination for Beginners

Discover the Techniques that Work for You

SCOTT CUNNINGHAM

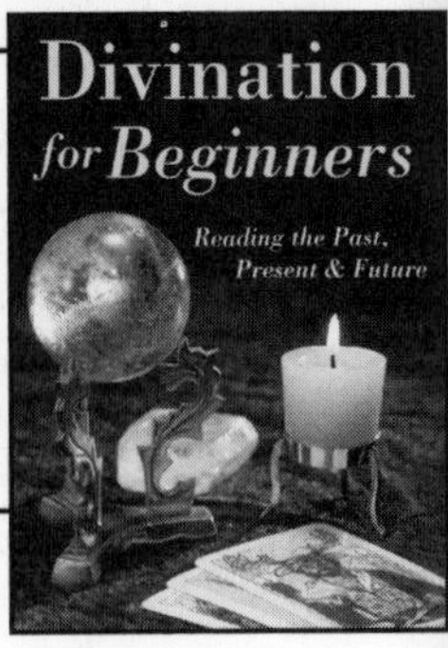

There's no need to visit a soothsayer or call a psychic hotline to glimpse into your future or to uncover your past. You can become your own diviner of things unseen with the many methods outlined in this book, written by popular author Scott Cunningham.

Here you will find detailed descriptions of both common and unusual divinatory techniques, each grouped by the tools or techniques used to perform them. Many utilize natural forces such as water, clouds, smoke, and the movement of birds. Also discussed are the more advanced techniques of Tarot, Palmistry, and the I Ching.

0-7387-0384-2, 28 pp., $5\frac{3}{16}$ x 8 **$9.95**

To order, call 1-877-NEW-WRLD

Prices subject to change without notice

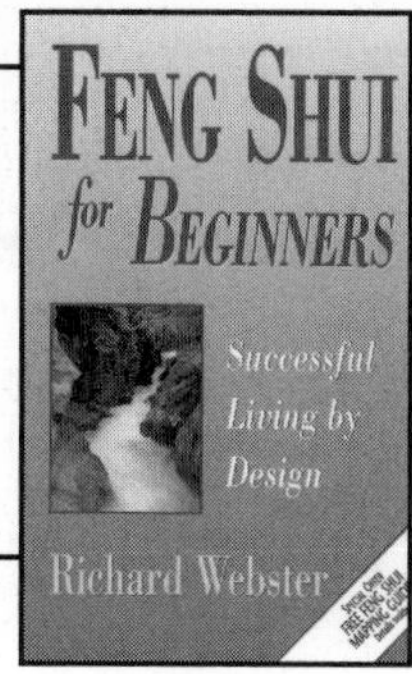
FENG SHUI
for BEGINNERS
Successful
Living by
Design
Richard Webster

Healing Alternatives for Beginners

Kay Henrion

HEALING ALTERNATIVES *for* BEGINNERS

Whole Body Approach to Health and Well Being

When someone begins to seek out alternative ways of healing, they encounter a deluge of confusing and often conflicting information on health, healing modalities, foods, and supplements, even from the practitioners themselves.

This book, written by a registered nurse, gives people a starting place for their journey into taking responsibility for their own health. It answers questions in layman's language regarding meditation and visualization, diets and vitamins, herbs, homeopathy, therapeutic touch, the aging process, AIDS, even natural healing for pets. It is full of anecdotes and examples from the author's own life and the lives of her patients.

1-56718-427-8, 264 pp., 5 3/16 x 8 **$12.95**

To order, call 1-877-NEW-WRLD

Prices subject to change without notice

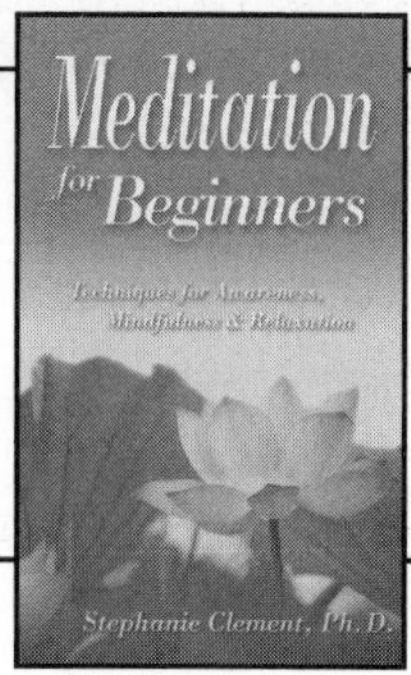

Meditation for Beginners

Techniques for Awareness, Mindfulness & Relaxation

STEPHANIE CLEMENT, PH.D.

Break the barrier between your conscious and unconscious minds.

Perhaps the greatest boundary we set for ourselves is the one between the conscious and less conscious parts of our own minds. We all need a way to gain deeper understanding of what goes on inside our minds when we are awake, asleep, or just not paying attention. Meditation is one way to pay attention long enough to find out.

Meditation for Beginners explores many different ways to meditate—including kundalini yoga, walking meditation, dream meditation, tarot meditations, and healing meditation—and offers a step-by-step approach to meditation, with exercises that introduce you to the rich possibilities of this age-old spiritual practice. Improve concentration, relax your body quickly and easily, work with your natural healing ability, and enhance performance in sports and other activities. Just a few minutes each day is all that's needed.

0-7387-0203-X, 264 pp., $5\frac{3}{16}$ x 8, illus. $12.95

To order, call 1-877-NEW-WRLD

Prices subject to change without notice

Palm Reading for Beginners

Find the Future in the Palm of Your Hand

RICHARD WEBSTER

Announce in any gathering that you read palms and you will be flocked by people thrilled to show you their hands. When you are have finished *Palm Reading for Beginners,* you will be able to look at anyone's palm (including your own) and confidently and effectively tell them about their personality, love life, hidden talents, career options, prosperity, and health.

Palmistry is possibly the oldest of the occult sciences, with basic principles that have not changed in 2,600 years. This step-by-step guide clearly explains the basics, as well as advanced research conducted in the past few years on such subjects as dermatoglyphics.

1-56718-791-9, 264 pp., 5³⁄₁₆ x 8, illus. **$9.95**

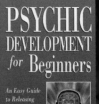

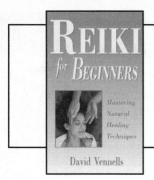

Spiritualism & Clairvoyance for Beginners

Simple Techniques to Develop Your Psychic Abilities

Elizabeth Owens

Margaretta and Catherine Fox's successful communication with a spirit entity in 1848 sparked a new understanding of the spirit world in the United States. This new movement is called Modern Spiritualism. Based on Spiritualism's rich tradition, Elizabeth Owens demonstrates how one can develop natural clairvoyant skills in order to hear the "wisdom of the spirits."

Emphasizing patience and practice, the author insists that clairvoyance is possible for everyone. She explains many forms of clairvoyance (psychometry, clairsentience, clairaudience, and so on), and offers examples based on her own experiences and those of six other spiritualist mediums. Exercises in meditation, memory development, visualization, and symbol interpretation progressively help readers enhance and cultivate their own innate gift of the "sixth sense."

0-7387-0707-4, 192 pp., 5¾₆ x 8 **$10.95**

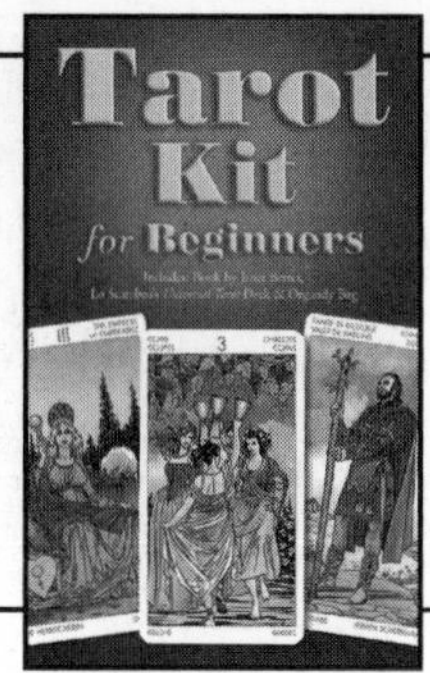

Tarot Kit for Beginners

Book by Janet Berres:

Your Guide to the Tarot

Includes Lo Scarabeo's

Universal Tarot deck

Here's the first step to becoming a Tarot pro! More and more people are drawn to the Tarot for its captivating artwork and uncanny ability to guide us toward personal insight. Yet, newcomers often feel intimidated by this historic divination tool. *Llewellyn's Tarot Kit for Beginners* is designed for those who wish to embark on the exhilarating journey of Tarot reading.

Packed with wisdom and knowledge acquired by accomplished Tarot practitioner Janet Berres, the enclosed guidebook also explains the basics, such as choosing decks, deciphering card meanings, and working with spreads. Readers will learn the history of Tarot, the traditional structure of the deck, and the truth behind common Tarot myths.

0-7387-0506-3, **$19.95**
Kit includes 216-page book, 78 full-color cards

To order, call 1-877-NEW-WRLD

Prices subject to change without notice

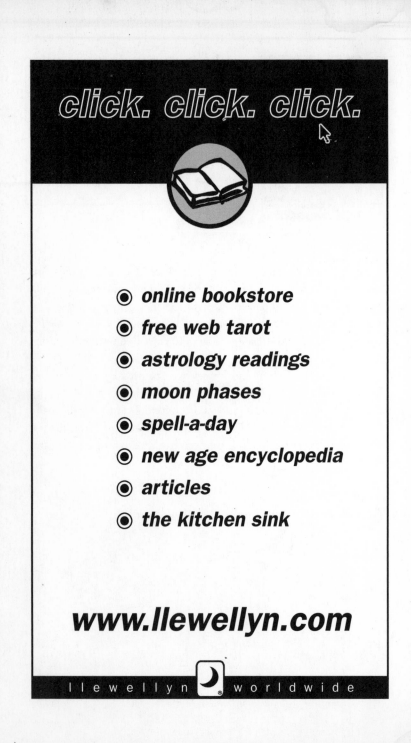